THESE TWELVE DAYS

THESE TWELVE DAYS

A FAMILY GUIDE TO AFTER-CHRISTMAS CELEBRATIONS

JAMES KASPERSON &
MARINA D. LACHECKI

United Church Press   Cleveland, Ohio

United Church Press, Cleveland, Ohio 44115
© 1999 by James Kasperson and Marina D. Lachecki

Biblical quotations are from the New Revised Standard Version of the Bible,
© 1989 by the Division of Christian Education of the National Council of
the Churches of Christ in the U.S.A., and are used by permission. Adapted
for inclusivity.

Printed in China on acid-free paper

04   03   02   01   00   99   5   4   3   2   1

Library of Congress Cataloging-in-Publication Data

Kasperson, James.
    These twelve days : a family guide to after-Christmas celebrations /
James Kasperson and Marina D. Lachecki.
        p.   cm.
    Includes bibliographical references and indexes.
    ISBN 0-8298-1316-0 (pbk. : alk. paper)
    1. Christmas.   2. Epiphany.   I. Lachecki, Marina.   II. Title.
BV45.K37   1999
263'.915—dc21   98-54174
                                                                    CIP

To

*our parents, who raised us in an
environment where sacred and cultural traditions
were central to the Christmas season.*

To

*every child who counts the days
of Advent waiting for the magic and
mystery of Christmas.*

To

*the God who affirmed all of
creation by entering our physical
world at Christmas.*

CONTENTS

—

—

PREFACE

In the middle of the last decade, one of us was called to serve a new congregation in northern Wisconsin. The call began in July, and things proceeded normally until a few weeks before Thanksgiving. It was then that the Christmas/Advent battle began. The congregation had been served by a pastor who actively promoted the celebration of Advent and who discouraged the celebration of Christmas until the evening of December 24.

As is often the case, congregation members began to identify themselves as with the pastor or against the pastor. In this case that translated as pro-Advent people and pro-Christmas people. The fighting focused on issues such as whether to sing Christmas carols in the Advent season and whether to defer decorating the tree until Christmas Eve. It seemed that every observance of either season had been polarized. The new pastor in the parish walked through a minefield each day of the season. By the time Christmas Day came, pastor and congregation alike were relieved to drop the Christmas issue and let things drift passively and peacefully toward the secular celebration of the New Year.

This unhappy scenario is not unique. Christian people are often torn between the traditional church season of Advent and the secular expectation of celebrating Christmas between Thanksgiving and Christmas Day. Either approach represents a loss. This book began as a response to this situation.

We recognize the importance of celebrating Advent: a season of preparation, expectation, and hope. Yet we also acknowledge that the Christmas holiday is important enough to celebrate for more than an eve and a day. Thus, we searched the traditions of both the Eastern church and the Western church, looking for those lost twelve days (known to many only as a song of turtle doves and five golden rings). We were surprised to discover the depth, the variety, and the importance of the celebration of these traditional days.

This book is an attempt to share with you some of the richness of that tradition.

ACKNOWLEDGMENTS

—

We were raised in families where special Christmas foods and ethnic traditions contributed to the joy of the sacred season. For Jim, it was a Scandinavian Christmas Eve dinner of oyster stew and lutefisk followed by the reading of the Christmas story by the Christmas tree. For Marina, it was attending the Midnight Mass of the Shepherds followed by a Polish sausage "early morning" breakfast and the sharing of the peace wafer, the *opatik*. These traditions were passed down for generations, and we offer a word of gratitude to our ancestors for carrying on the Christmas story in such rich ways.

As pastors and members of various churches throughout our lives, we appreciate the Christian tradition and its many expressions of Christmas festivities: Christmas chorales and pageants, Vespers, and ethnic celebrations on holy days.

As the idea for this book began to take shape, we became indebted to the staff and patrons of the Washburn Public Library and to the Lutheran Church Women at First Lutheran in Port Wing, who listened to our stories and research during two holiday seasons.

We especially thank Dick Bruesehoff and Peg Augustine, who offered words of encouragement at critical times.

We appreciate the support and enthusiasm for this work expressed by our congregations, First Lutheran Church in Port Wing, and St. John's United Church of Christ on Madeline Island.

Two of our chapter ideas were published in anthologies. We appreciate Routledge Press and Dimensions for Living for giving voice and support to our concepts.

Finally, we share a deep sense of gratitude to Kim Sadler and United Church Press for bringing this book to light. You recognized our dream and enabled us to share this message with other families.

INTRODUCTION

—

Twelve days, twelve nights: the season of Christmas. *These Twelve Days* is a book about Christmas, of God coming into the world. It is a book written for families, communities, and congregations to share the stories and traditions of times past as well as rituals and stories of today.

These twelve holy days were celebrated long before the Christchild was born. The Romans gathered to observe the birthday of the Unconquered Sun at the time of the winter solstice. During this time between Saturnalia and Calends, candles were lit and presents exchanged as tokens of cheerfulness and goodwill.

The Jewish Feast of the Dedication came near the time of Saturnalia. Historians believe that thousands of candles were burning brightly through Palestine at the time of Christ's birth. First-century Christians adopted this period to celebrate the light of God coming into the world. Twelve days were set aside, with the first and last days being celebrated with great solemnity as the Greater and Lesser Epiphany, December 25 and January 6.

Each day of the twelve days that follow Christmas has a history, a tradition, and a story, from the Feast of Stephen to the Feast of the Holy Family, from the scripture stories of Mary and Joseph to those of the holy innocents and the Magi. With this presentation of the twelve days of Christmas, we draw from the traditions and rituals of Western and Eastern Orthodox churches, and ethnic celebrations affiliated with the days.

Based on the scripture readings as laid out in the Revised Common Lectionary, each chapter carries a theme of the Old or New Testament lesson. After a brief introduction, a story—suitable for reading aloud to others or individually in silence—begins each chapter's exploration. Next, a tradition section presents background information on the religious and cultural traditions of that day; it can be read ahead of time to share verbally after a family or group reading of the story. Each chapter concludes with "Entering the Ritual: Ideas for Family Celebration." If you have some time, pick one as a group and enjoy further exploring that particular day of the Christmas celebration.

These Twelve Days shares with you the days of Christmas. It elaborates their traditions and suggests ways to celebrate them as families, congregations, and communities of friends. And it presents stories that will help you experience the gift of each day.

1

CHRISTMAS DAY

Christmas Day: This day of the twelve is one we know well. The Festival of the Incarnation is the one day of the twelve that is celebrated by all Christians. Today in churches around the world, the miracle of God begotten human has been read and proclaimed: the story of the shepherds, the angels, the inn, the manger, Joseph and Mary.

As we reflect on the Christmas story, we focus the story of the Word, the very power that created everything. The Word that was from the beginning with God. The Word that is God. The Word through which all things were made. The very Word that "became flesh and dwelt among us."

This Christmas story is Genesis told anew. It is a story of total affirmation. God affirms the goodness and value of creation and creatures by entering them both. The incarnation speaks to God's love and affirmation for all of creation, from the handmaiden of God and her carpenter husband to the cave that held the oxen and ass. This miracle, this baby Jesus, was not only God in human form. This was God living and breathing in God's creation.

SCRIPTURE

John 1:1–5, 10–12, 14

In the beginning was the Word; and the Word was with God, and the Word was God. God was in the beginning with God. All things came

1

into being through God, and without God not one thing came into being. What has come into being in God was life, and the life was the light of all people. The light shines in the shadows, and the shadows did not overcome it. God was in the world, and the world came into being through God; yet the world did not know God. God came to what was God's own, and God's own people did not accept God. But to all who received God, who believed in God's name, power was given to become children of God. And the Word became flesh and lived among us, and we have seen God's glory, the glory as of a parent's only child, full of grace and truth.

CHRISTMAS DAWN

Norman brushed two inches of snow off the windshield of his car as he began his daily journey to the only café in town for his evening meal. The air was cold. The car groaned before it started. Snow was falling in light, small flakes. Norman drove the six blocks to the café and parked in back. He had eaten one meal a day here for the six years that had passed since Emma died. He always parked in the same place, sat at the same spot at the counter, and visited with the same people. It made him feel at home—like family. But today was different. Today he was two hours early for supper. The café closed at 4:00 P.M. today. Today was Christmas Eve.

Supper was the one daily time in Norman's life when he was not alone. The company was as important as the food. He walked in past the shipping crates in the back hall, past the kitchen, and headed to his spot at the counter. The restaurant was empty.

"Everyone must be already getting ready for the big night," Norman thought. "Maybe I'll go back and stand with Dick in the kitchen."

He walked back to the kitchen, rapped on the door, and stepped in. The odor of hash browns was a presence in this room, even when none were on the grill.

"What are you up to, Norman?" a man in white pants and T-shirt greeted him. "You're a little early today."

2

"I guess it's eat early today or never," Norman replied as he slipped up onto an empty counter. "You and everybody else have important things to do tonight. I'll take the hot beef sandwich."

As Dick went to the refrigerator, he said, "What's up for you for Christmas, Norm? Are you going down to your brother Ted's place?"

"Not until tomorrow," Norman replied. "It's such a long drive that I decided to stay home tonight. I've been alone on Christmas Eve before. These last five years I've gotten used to being alone."

The phone rang. Dick handed Norman his hot beef sandwich and a glass of milk as he answered the phone. Norman carried his meal out to the dining room and sat at the counter. Alone.

"It's not so bad," he told himself. "This really is a day like any other day. I'm eating early so I might as well just go to bed early. Next thing I know it'll be morning."

On his way home he stopped at the store for a few groceries. The store was all but deserted. The shelves were bare of groceries, and the aisles were bare of people. He was surprised at how early this little town shut down for Christmas. He drove slowly through town. It was dusk, and the lights of the homes were coming on. He looked in at each house with open drapes and imagined the smells.

"There is probably ham in some, turkey in others and roast beef. I remember the roast beef dinners . . . "

Norman pulled into the familiar garage, turned off the car, and walked through the darkness to the kitchen door. He'd lived here for thirty-five years and knew every step in the dark.

All of a sudden he heard a screech. At the same time, he felt something at his feet. He jumped, startled, and dropped his groceries. "The cat," he concluded. "It's that cat that's been hanging around here since Thursday. I thought she was gone. She's been in here."

As he picked up his groceries, he was thankful for the first time for the wax milk cartons. He had complained to Emma many times about missing the old glass bottles. Today he was glad for the carton—the glass would have broken.

In the kitchen he put away his groceries. He heard the cat again, outside the kitchen window. This time it was a simple meow, no screeching. He remembered cats. They'd had no children, but Emma always had two cats. When Norman was growing up, cats always belonged in the barn, not the house. But Emma's cats, they lived indoors. He'd never really complained to her, but he never really liked it. When she died, he gave them to Emma's niece.

He heard it again, "Meow." "She wants in. If I let her in, she'll never leave. I'll just go to bed. I won't hear her from the bedroom." Norman went to bed before 7 P.M., about three hours before his usual bedtime. As he went to sleep, he thought about Christmas. He thought about Emma and felt alone.

"Three in the morning—I should have known better. Go to bed three hours early, and wake up three hours early." Norman crawled out of bed and went down to the kitchen. The squeaking of the stairs sounded rude in the quiet, empty house.

"Christmas morning," he thought. "I'll fix some coffee and sit in the chair to wait for the dawn. If I leave now, I'll get to Ted's house too early."

Norman filled the coffee pot and sat at the table to wait

"Meow."

"There it is again. She still wants in."

It might have been that he wasn't quite awake. It might have been that he didn't have the heart to chase it away. It might have been the one more request that he could not refuse. He didn't know why, but Norman opened the kitchen door. The cold greeted his whole body.

"Here, Kitty," he called. "Here, Kitty. Come on in."

The cat responded immediately. Norman went to the refrigerator and took out the milk. "It's no thanks to you that I still have this milk," he reflected on his spill the evening before.

He poured the milk in the bowl and opened a can of tuna fish. As the cat enjoyed this fine meal, Norman drank his coffee.

He was tired and still felt alone. He went to the living room and sat in his chair. The cat soon joined him on his lap, licking her paws and getting the last of the tuna oil.

"Why do they always land on my lap?" he wondered as he remembered Emma's cats. Just as he was about to brush the cat off his leg, he felt its warmth. He let it stay for just a moment.

Then it started. The purr. It filled the room.

"They all purr alike," he remembered. The sound was warmth to him. It was company. It was history. He was not alone. And for that moment, it felt like Christmas again.

THE TRADITION

One of the most profound introductions to the celebration of Christmas occurs in monasteries at morning prayer. It begins:

> In the 5199th year of the creation of the world, from the time when God in the beginning created the heaven and the earth . . . and all the earth being at peace, Jesus Christ, the Eternal God, and Son of the Eternal Father, wishing to consecrate the world by His most merciful coming . . . was born in Bethlehem of Judea of the Virgin Mary, made human.[1]

This Christmas proclamation ties the beginning of the world with the renewing of the world in the birth of Jesus Christ. While the focus of the Christmas story has been on the people who witnessed this miracle, it is all of creation that was redeemed in Christ's coming. It is not known exactly when Jesus came into this world. But the traditional celebration of Christmas on December 25 was established in the fourth century. It occurred during the Jewish month of *Tishri,* in which festivals were held associated with creation and the renewal of the earth. During this time, the Roman empire also celebrated Saturnalia, which honored the god of plenty. The festival was instituted in honor of Noah, the real Saturnas, and dedicated to the family of humans and other creatures on the ark. The twelve days of Christmas developed from these roots. The time between December 25 (the winter solstice in the first centuries) and January 1 (the Roman New Year celebration of Calends) was revered as twelve holy days, and centuries later they were called the "twelve holy nights."

People in these bygone years believed that animals and plants shared in the joy of humanity on Christmas Day, which became a day of salvation for the whole of creation. The honoring of animals and birds had many expressions in northern Europe. Farmers believed that the animals that ate from the manger stood out at midnight in honor of Christ's birth. Rural folk from Sweden, Norway, Denmark, Poland, Germany, and Hungary would make sure the sheep, horses, and oxen would have special food and attention on that holy night. It continues to be a tradition among those people to place sheaves of grain atop barn eaves, chimneys, and on tall poles in the middle of the barnyard for the birds to feast on.

In the mountains of Assisi in northern Italy, another Christmas animal tradition was created in the twelfth century. Saint Francis of Assisi lived in the Sabiner Mountains. He saw God's handiwork in all of creation. On a snowy Christmas Eve, he thought to celebrate the story of Jesus' birth in a new way: He gathered farm animals in a cave in the mountains, took a manger, and filled it with hay. He invited nearby villagers to come and worship, much like the angels bid the shepherds to come on a Christmas evening in Bethlehem. Peasants and local shepherds came up snowy paths, carrying torches to behold the first living manger. Francis then told the farmers to give their oxen and asses extra corn and hay at Christmas time, instructing them that all creation should rejoice at Christmas. The manger—now so common in our Christmas households—stands as the witness of all creation, from the beasts of burden to the angel choirs, to the salvation of the newborn Christ.

ENTERING THE STORY: IDEAS FOR FAMILY CELEBRATION

How does one enter into the miracle of the Christmas story? In many ways, you already have. Like Joseph and Mary you prepared for this event. You may have traveled to be with family or close friends. No doubt family rituals are repeated each year as the day of Christ's birth draws near. Special foods are eaten, traditional songs sung, and worship services attended.

After your Christmas dinner today, or perhaps as your family approaches the end of its day together, take a few moments to reflect on the Word of God, which created the world and saw that it was good; the Word of life, which came to be with God's creation on this day two thousand years ago.

1. What traditions does your family keep on Christmas? Where did those rituals start? How were they taught or handed down?

2. What are your memories of past rituals or family Christmas stories?

3. Recount the Christmas story: the star of Bethlehem, the angel choirs, the shepherds, the animals in the stable, the holy family—all parts of the creation which came to honor the Creator's coming into the world.

4. How have the traditions your family keeps been an expression of the Word made flesh? Of love and Creator entering creation?

5. As a final activity to this day, bring out bowls of popcorn and cranberries to string for the animals and birds in your yard or in a nearby park. Hang tidbits of bread, suet logs, pine cones spread with peanut butter and bird seed. Extend the joy of Christmas to all of creation.

2

THE FEAST OF STEPHEN

—

December 26

Today is the second day of Christmas. On this day we turn away from family gatherings and turn toward the communities in which we live. This day has traditionally been one in which the spirit of Christmas, God's unconditional love for creation, is carried toward the world which God created. The Middle Ages brought the practice of setting out poor boxes in churches. Today's extension of that act of charity is seen in gifts being distributed on this day to those who have served us throughout the year—mail carriers, health-care providers, employees.

Turning away from our own family festivities and to our neighbors is one way in which we bear the Christchild to the world. On this day we hear the story of how one individual— Saint Stephen, who lived in the first century of the Christian era—modeled this nature, and of how a medieval king, Wenceslas, celebrated Stephen's servanthood.

Like this good King Wenceslas,[1] we look out on the Feast of Stephen and become God-bearers to the world.

SCRIPTURE

Acts 6:8
Stephen, full of grace and power, did great wonders and signs among the people.

ON THE FEAST

"A king's page?" My brother laughed the words back to me after I told him about my new job. "Imagine my brother Vavrina masquerading as a king's page."

I looked to the others in the room for support. My mother looked interested but apprehensive. I might have known that my brother Val would not take this new job of mine seriously. He never thought anything about me was serious. "I will be with King Wenceslas almost twenty-four hours a day. If I do a good job, who can predict what future power will come my way?"

Val stirred the fire in the corner hearth. "And who can predict how long the king will let you live when you fail him with one of your coughing attacks?"

He spoke my fears aloud. I'd had the attacks since I was a child. One moment I would breath fine, and the next I would feel like someone had cinched a saddle too tightly around my chest. The more deeply I would try to breathe, the tighter the saddle. "I haven't had one of those for years," I answered. My mother looked away with worry. I breathed deeply and assured them all. "I've outgrown those spells. They are the burden of children. I am twenty-one years a man."

Val laughed again. I would always be a child to him.

It had all started with the king's brother Boleslav. Daily he was seen on the streets surrounding the castle. He would strike out with the power of the kingdom at the slightest provocation. No one was immune to the judgment of Boleslav.

It was an early summer morning, and I was in the market looking for flour for my mother. I spotted "Brother Bol," as the townspeople called him, near the castle entrance to the market square. He strolled into the square, sampling the merchants' wares as if he owned them all. He thought he did. I stayed on the other side of the square, preferring to avoid any encounter with the power of the king's family. The word on the street was that the king was good, but my only contact had been through his brother. It didn't seem good to me.

"You will never find flour for less, my friend Vavrina," Czeslaw the miller replied to my offer of two kopecks for the bag. "I will need three to even cover the labor of grinding."

Before I could agree with what I knew to be a fair price for the flour, a shout came from the castle side of the square. Brother Bol was standing in a wagon that was hitched to two horses. As he shouted out a count, he tossed pumpkins one by one from the wagon. The owner of the wagon just stood mute. "You call these food?" Bol screamed. "Just one more pile of pulp and seeds for the pigs!" He tossed the last one off the wagon, calling out "nine." He then smacked the rear of the nearest horse with his hand and sent the team careening through the square. The horses headed for the home side market entrance. As I watched the horses approach, I realized that they were headed directly for a small boy who was playing with wood scraps in the square. Before I could think of anything, including the justice of Bol, I stepped out and stopped the horses before they reached the boy. A man standing next to me sucked air in and whispered, "He saw you do that. He'll deal with you next."

He was right. Bol was looking at me. Just when I thought he was starting to come my way, he stopped, turned, and left the square.

"You seem to be handy with horses," someone said, placing a hand on my shoulder. I turned to see a man who was a head again larger than I, dressed in clean but simple clothes. I'd never seen him in the town, but he spoke as if he was at home. "Your king could use a man like you. Come to the castle gates at dawn," he continued. "I'll fix you up with a job."

Before I could reply, he was gone. He must have come from the castle, I concluded.

I was in for a surprise in the morning. As I approached the castle I was worried about meeting the king—so worried that I even felt short of breath. At the door of the castle an old man, barely able to walk, met me. He wore the colors of the king's guard, but he was not armed.

I introduced myself, "I am Vavrina. A man told me to call at the castle this morning."

He nodded. "Follow me. I am Zack, the king's page."

We walked through a great hall, filled with three long wooden tables. As we climbed a cold stony staircase, Zack turned and instructed me, "Take off your hat. You will now meet your king."

As I removed my hat, he opened the door. There he was: The plain man from the market. He was the king.

He spoke simply. "I need another page to help Zack. You are that man."

I worked for him for those first few months without a problem. I stayed next to him whenever he left his private chambers. I saw Brother Bol only once during that time. The other stewards said that he spent most of his time in his own quarters in the east wing. I saw him one time, when the king was preparing to leave the castle for a visit to his uncle nearby. He visited Bol in the east wing before he left. He asked me to accompany him. I stood back in the shadows as Bol spoke to the king from the door of his chambers. I was afraid that he would recognize me from the market. My chest tightened with fear at the very sight of him. The king spoke in a soft voice while Bol simply nodded and looked at the earthen floor of the hallway. I turned away throughout their conversation, but as their conversation came to a close, he caught my eye. I was safe, only because I worked for the king. I fell in behind the king as we walked back to the west wing.

I liked this king. He was strong and fair. He knew the way of power. One could see his power whenever he dealt with Bol or others in the heart of his reign. Yet, I never felt his power as much as I felt his presence. When I was with him, he did not have to look at me to claim my attention or to know what I was doing. He simply had it and knew it. I was happy to serve him.

Each day began with mass. The king had a private chapel in the castle, but he attended daily mass at the cathedral. The Christ mass marked the beginning of my fourth month with the king. After mass, we returned to the great hall for a day of feasting.

When the final toast was made, we retired for the evening. The king caught me as I was leaving the hall. "Come early tomorrow, Vavrina. It is the Feast of Stephen, we have much work to do. We need to carry this Christmas feast to the people of our land."

Nuts and fruit. It was a day of nuts and fruit from lands far away. We carried baskets of them to the market and gave them away. We carried more to homes at the edge of town. We made trip after trip to the castle for more baskets. As the people accepted the gifts, they recognized my attire as the livery of the king, but they did not recognize the king.

"Simple man, probably a helper," they must have thought as their own king served them with Christmas cheer. I was exhausted as we headed back to the castle at the end of the day.

"It has been a good day of Stephen," King Wenceslas said as we walked together. As we approached the market, a man crossed the snowy square. He was gathering scraps of wood from discarded crates in the market to use as firewood for his home.

"Who is that man, Vavrina?" the king asked.

I'd seen him before. "He lives way out underneath the mountain. Out near the edge of forest by St. Agnes fountain."

The king looked back toward the man, who was now heading toward the forest. "Our work is not done. We shall gather a feast and carry it to this man."

The snow was still falling as we left the castle for what I hoped was the last trip of the day. We carried fruit and flesh, a feast that would feed a family for a month. The snow piled high, and each of my steps felt as if it demanded the last bit of my energy. As the village lights dimmed in the falling snow behind us, I felt it: the saddle tightening around my chest. The burden of my youth was with me still.

I stopped beside the king, unable to lift my feet in the snow. It was now here, my last day as a page. I could hear my brother's words, "And who can predict how long the king will let you live when you fail him with one of your coughing attacks?"

I simply couldn't breath. I thought of Boleslav and imagined what he would do to me if the king released me from his services.

The king stopped and silently let me rest. When my breathing returned, he said, "Follow me." He walked ahead, leaving a trail of footprints for me to follow. The walk was easy. I knew that my job was safe. This king accepted me, even with this childhood burden. This Wenceslas was a good king.

THE TRADITION

"Good King Wenceslas looked out on the Feast of Stephen." How often is this Christmas carol sung without knowing that both Stephen and Wenceslas were historic figures? Stephen lived in the first century and was called to care for the needy of his time, the widows. From the fourth century on, it was his work among the community that was celebrated on the first day of the Christmas season. Stephen, along with John the evangelist and the holy innocents, were designated as *comites Christi,* friends of Christ. It is their feasts that mark the beginning of the Christmas season. Each, in their own way, brought Christ to the world.

During the Middle Ages, a number of traditions arose that marked this day as one to provide for the poor and needy. Poor boxes were left in churches where the wealthy could share their fortunes with the poor. This custom is known as "Boxing Day" in Great Britain, Canada, and Australia. Christmas boxes are sent to those who render services to the public at large: clerks, apprentices, employees, mail carriers, health-care workers, and other civil servants. No doubt it was this custom to which King Wenceslas, a tenth-century Bohemian king, subscribed. As the legend goes, Wenceslas lived simply, dressed plainly, and shared whatever he had, like the food, fuel, and drink in the song, with the people he ruled—especially on December 25 and 26.

The custom of sharing gifts on this day dates back to the ancient Romans, who practiced gift-giving as part of their observance of Saturnalia. Eventually, the idea was linked to the work of Stephen and grew over the centuries. The practice of sending a gift to a favorite charity also grew out of this feast. In Ireland, the event is called "Feeding the Wren." It is based on a legend that Stephen was hiding in a furze bush (an Old World evergreen) and was betrayed to his enemies by a songbird. Irish children gather together and place a wren in a cage on top of a furze bush. Then they travel from door to door, carrying the bird, to collect money for charity.

In other European countries, the Feast of Stephen marked the beginning of a time of rest for domestic animals. Horses, as the most useful servant of humans during the Middle Ages, were accorded honor on this first night of the Christmas season. Farmers decorated their horses with wreaths (the name Stephen means "wreath" in Greek) and brought them to a priest to be blessed. After the blessing, the whole family would take a wagon or sleigh ride. The horses' food (oats), water, and salt (used to heal horses when they were sick) were also blessed on this day.

In a number of ways, the Feast of Stephen calls us to bring the joy and love of the Christmas season beyond the walls of our homes into a world that awaits its Redeemer. On this day, we have an opportunity to become God-bearers, like Stephen and Wenceslas, to all parts of creation.

ENTERING THE STORY: IDEAS FOR FAMILY CELEBRATION

The gift of Christmas is the gift of giving to others. The Feast of Stephen provides an opportunity to celebrate this aspect of the Christmas season. On this first day, look out beyond the doors of your home to the needs of the world around you with the following activities.

1. Make homemade gifts (baked goods, handmade ornaments) to give to those who have taken care of you this year: doctors, nurses, mail carriers, day-care workers, teachers, and auto mechanics.

2. Sing the carol "Good King Wenceslas" after your evening meal. Find out where Bohemia is on a map and talk about the days of kings and serfs.

3. Honor the pets in your life by decorating them with a Christmas bow or wreath. Bring them a special meal or buy them a new toy.

4. If your community has people who work with draught horses, find out if you can arrange a sleigh ride for members of your family or for close friends. Dash through the snow on a one-horse open sleigh.

5. As a family, discuss what local charity you will support during the coming year. Adopt it for one year, and give a gift of money or labor on other holidays: Valentine's Day, your birthday, Easter, Independence Day, Halloween, and Thanksgiving.

6. Go Christmas caroling at a nursing home. Organize a 4-H group, a scout troop, or a group of neighborhood children to join you. Have each family bring Christmas treats to share with the residents.

3

The Feast of Saint John

—

December 27

Before creation, there was emptiness. Out of emptiness, God created and brought forth life. Before the resurrection, there was obscurity—the obscurity of the tomb. Out of that obscurity, God redeemed and renewed the face of the earth.

On the third day of Christmas, we celebrate the life and works of John the evangelist. The gospel story John wrote did not begin with the manger and the shepherds. John connected the story of Jesus' birth to the dawn of creation. In the beginning was the Word. In the Gospel of John, the creative power of the Word continues to the resurrection and from the resurrection throughout all of history.

The apostle John spoke of salvation coming to all of God's created world. The gospel story we read this day is not of the incarnation but of that Word enfleshed on the cross and risen from the dead, of the God who brought life to the world, who redeemed the world by dying and rising from the dead. The Feast of Saint John celebrates the story of Immanuel, God through us, with us, and in us. The Word continually made flesh in the world.

SCRIPTURE

1 John 1:1–2

We declare to you what was from the beginning, what we have heard, what we have seen with our eyes, what we have looked at and touched with our hands, concerning the word of life—this life was revealed, and we have seen it and testify to it and declare to you the eternal life that was with God and was revealed to us.

VINCE'S DREAM

Vince was not a dreamer. His shoe repair shop was certainly not a dream. It was at the bottom of a stairwell, recessed into the sidewalk of a city street that was mostly vacant these days. Once, when Vince was learning the trade from Vincent Popich Sr., the street was busy. Apartments were the homes of middle-class families, stores did a good business, and life on this street was going somewhere. Not today. Few people walked the sidewalks above his shop. Despite the condition of the neighborhood, his business did well. People drove in from the suburbs to get their shoes fixed. They had no choice. Suburban shoemakers were rare. So Vince stayed in the old building. He had a room upstairs. It was handy.

Life for Vince was lived on this street, between the shop, Tiny's Café, which was three storefronts toward the avenue, and his apartment upstairs. He saw few people. The customers didn't stay long, always looking tense and anxious to get back into their cars. Besides them, his only worry was the stairwell. It seemed crazy to him because the street was almost always empty, but it was hard to keep the stairwell clear of people. Every morning he would leave his apartment, walk down the front stairs, go around to the side, and check the stairwell before descending to open his shop.

Drunks slept there. Vince supposed that they were harmless, but he was afraid of them anyway. When he found someone sleeping there, he would walk around to the back of the stairwell, lean over the rail, and yell. That rarely worked. Then he would drop cans or whatever he could find on the street. He didn't aim to hurt them—just wake them up. Once a man woke up swinging. Vince was glad to be clear of the stairwell.

Then there were the kids. Vince couldn't figure out where they came from. No kids lived in his building. Wherever they came from, he wished they would stay there. They could figure out all kinds of reasons to come down the stairs. They would hide down there, chase the balls that constantly found their way down, and hang on the railing. The more he chased them away, the more they came.

Vince was not a dreamer, but last night he had a dream. At least he thought it was a dream. As he opened the door to the shop, he remembered: He'd had an angel beside his bed. He believed in angels, although he had not been in a church for years. When he was younger and his parents took him to church, he used to squint at the angels on the windows and pretend that they were moving. He had always remembered the story of the angel visiting Mary. As a child, he had expected such a visit someday. Once it had seemed to Vince that he was special and that such a visit was entirely reasonable. Now, when he had given up on angels for years, an angel had actually visited his room. At first, he thought he was dying. Then he decided that he was dreaming.

The angel spoke a simple promise, "The Savior is going to visit your shop, Vince. Be ready."

Vince called out to wake himself from the dream, but he was already sitting on the side of the bed. He sat there a moment, noticed the early light of dawn entering through the one window, and decided to head down to Tiny's for an early breakfast.

He decided to forget the dream, but he couldn't. It stayed with him as he continued the routine of opening his shop. He checked the opening balance in the cash register. The idea of God seemed real to him again. He examined the shoes on his "to-do" shelf, looking for the oldest order with which to start. The dream made him feel special, but it was just a dream. Vince decided to enjoy the momentary pleasure of the feeling and forget about it.

In the middle of a leather resole job, the world entered his doorstep in the form of a basketball. This one hit the window, startling him before it settled in the corner.

"I'm going to lose a window someday," he concluded as he headed to the door to grab the ball. When balls hit the window, he would grab them and keep them in his back room. He had two shipping crates full of an assortment of stray balls.

Just as he opened the door, a young girl with a green parka and no mittens bounded down the stairs. She spotted Vince when she was about halfway down, but her momentum carried her past him to the bottom of the steps. Vince stepped out, and the girl was trapped. Their eyes met for a moment, and then Vince looked downward quickly. He simply could not bear to confront the fear in her eyes. He spotted the ball, reached past her to pick it up, and then handed it to her. She hesitated at first, not daring to reach toward this man she feared.

Vince then surprised himself. He handed her the ball, opened the door, and said in a voice that sounded foreign to him, "Get your friends and come back to my shop. I have something for you." She slipped by him, making the escape that moments ago looked impossible, and ran up the stairs.

"Please come back with your friends," he called after her. "You won't be in trouble." Vince shut the door behind him and went back to the leather soles. He knew that he wanted the kids to come back, he just didn't understand why. He didn't have time to wonder. He heard a rap on the window that opened to the staircase. She must have needed the strength of numbers, because she now stood in the little stairwell with more than a half-dozen children. They stood and looked in at him. He stood and looked out. Then Vince turned to the back room. He slid out one shipping crate filled with balls—from tennis balls to basket-balls—and turned to get the other. With both crates in place, he motioned for the kids to come in.

His first young friend stepped in, and Vince bounced a basketball her way. She passed it back, and instantly there appeared an assembly line of recovered balls. Baseballs, footballs, soccer balls, and more. One by one they passed from Vince to the hands of their original owners or in some cases, the children of the original owners. This affair continued without a word until the sidewalk was covered with balls. He handed his young friend the remaining two baseball caps and a tennis racquet and then spoke his first words, "Now be gone."

She turned back toward him as she left the shop and said simply, "Thank you."

There were no promises and no explanations. As the door swung shut, he heard the sound of balls bouncing. Vince surprised himself. He smiled. Then he continued to sole and resole throughout the day. He listened for bouncing balls.

The next morning, he found another sleeper. He stood at the top of the stairs and shouted. It worked this time. The man stood up immediately and looked up at Vince. Fear. There was the same fear in his eyes that Vince had seen in the little girl.

"You look cold," Vince said again in a voice that he did not recognize as his own. "Come in and have some warm coffee," he continued. "I've got some doughnuts."

He opened the door and guided the sleeper to the only chair in the shop. The man moved the chair closer to the heat vent. Now that he had him in the shop, Vince didn't know what to do next.

The man solved the problem. "Got anything else to eat?" he asked as he finished his doughnut. Vince had no other food, but he had an idea.

"I'll write a note for Tiny down the street. Take it to him, and I'll pay your bill when I get there for lunch," Vince said, feeling happy to have figured out a way to get the man out of his shop again. He quickly scribbled a note to Tiny, signed it, and watched the man as he ascended the staircase.

The days of deep winter were poor for Vince's business, so he busied himself cleaning the shop. As he worked, it occurred to him that it was almost as if he were getting ready for company.

Then he remembered the dream again. "Whatever you do to the least of these, you do to me," he recalled from somewhere in his past. "That's it," he concluded. "That is what the dream meant. The sleeper and the kids. That's what they were to me."

Vince shook his head and sat down. "Isn't that just like religion," he continued. "God Almighty comes to see you, and it costs you money." He returned to his cleaning, wishing that no one else would come to his shop today.

His wish was granted. He spent the rest of the day alone. He sat alone at Tiny's and went home to be alone. Sleep was a mercy that night, an interrupted mercy. Vince opened his eyes, and his angel was back. He sat up. He knew it was a dream, and he was angry. "Are you back with more promises?" he asked the angel. "Save them. I can't afford it. The Savior came to my shop all right, and it cost me money," he added, wondering where he got the courage to talk to an angel this way.

"Vince," the angel said gently. "God has indeed visited your shop as I promised, but I believe that you missed God."

Vince interrupted, "Oh, I saw God all right, in 'the least of these.'"

The angel responded, "You're right. God is to be found in those such as the children and the homeless, but the Savior you missed was found elsewhere." The angel stopped and looked directly at Vince.

Vince was stumped. He tried to remember everyone who visited the shop since the angel's first visit. There was no one who qualified. Nothing special had happened.

"It was through you, Vince. God came to the children when they received a fresh start with their balls. Your sleeper? He was fed freely and cared for. God visited your shop through you, Vince."

With that, Vince's angel was gone. He was wide awake, long before dawn. "Was that a dream?" he wondered as he opened his shop. "Was it a real angel?" He picked up a shoe and began to work.

A ball bounced down the staircase.[1]

THE TRADITION

Since the Middle Ages, the three days following Christmas have been set aside to honor the *comites Christi:* Saint Stephen, Saint John, and the holy innocents. These "companions of Christ" were held in highest esteem because they gave their lives for Christ or offered all they had for Christ to work within them for the sake of the world. Stephen was a deacon in the early years following Christ's death and resurrection. The holy innocents were children who were killed by Herod in his mania to destroy the threat to his power. John was the beloved disciple who gave his life and his gift of writing to sharing the good news of the Word made flesh.

On this third day of the Christmas season, we celebrate the life and works of John the apostle. He was part of Jesus' inner circle, which also included James and Peter. Together they witnessed Jesus' transfiguration, the healing of Jairus' daughter, and Christ's agony in the Garden of Gethsemane. John stood with the women at the foot of the cross and was given the care of Mary, the mother of God. John witnessed both the power of gloom as Jesus died on the cross and the power of life as the empty tomb revealed God's redemption of the world God created.

But it is within the legends of John's attempted executions and escapes that the traditions of this day are born. John traveled throughout Asia Minor preaching the gospel. He was accused of subverting the religion of Rome and was sentenced to boil in a cauldron of oil. He escaped unharmed.

At another time, John was offered poisoned wine. He drank it but did not die. During the Middle Ages, people in central Europe celebrated that story by bringing wine to their churches to be blessed. They took the wine home and poured a little of the blessed wine into each barrel of wine in their cellars. On the Feast of Saint John, people raised their glasses and toasted "Drink to the love of Saint John." The love toast was also shared at family weddings, with travelers before a long journey, and as a libation for the dying. The wine became a means of ritualizing both life and death, of remembering God's presence at the wedding feast at Cana, and at the Last Supper.

The love of Saint John was also extended to children at Christmas. Children with the name of John or its female counterpart, Joan, had the privilege of lighting the candles on Advent wreaths or the Christmas tree, remembering that Christ is the light of the world, as Jesus proclaimed himself to be in John's gospel.

The symbol most closely linked with Saint John is the eagle. In other cultures, the eagle is a sign of vision. It is the vision of John's gospel that is memorialized on this day. The God who brought life to the world with the sound of the divine voice redeemed that world with Jesus' death and resurrection. It seems unusual to consider the resurrection of Jesus in the midst of our celebration of his incarnation at Christmas. To do so affirms the wholeness of God's salvation. God continually breathes into and dwells within all of creation.

ENTERING THE STORY: IDEAS FOR FAMILY CELEBRATION

On the Feast of Saint John, we celebrate the living Word of God in the world today. Our God is one who continually makes the divine presence known throughout the universe, in all elements of creation. We honor a God who came to redeem the world in the new life born in Jesus' incarnation and through Jesus' death and resurrection.

1. Gather your family before the youngest child goes to bed. Name those people you have known to be friends of Christ, those who have shown care like Saint John or Saint Stephen. Say a thanksgiving prayer for them and their lives.

2. Find the words to the Easter hymn "Jesus Christ Is Risen Today" and celebrate the connection of the incarnation and the resurrection by singing those words to the Christmas carol, "Angels We Have Heard on High." The Easter hymn "Now The Green Blade Rises" is already set to an ancient French Christmas carol, *"Noël Nouvelet."*

3. During a family meal today, make a toast to Saint John with a special holiday punch. Remember the spirit of the person and his message: God's presence continually dwelling among us.

4. Purchase several tulip, crocus, and daffodil bulbs. Plant them in flower pots. With careful watering and tending, the flowers will emerge and bloom by Easter. As the flowers grow, remember that

at Easter we celebrate the final actions of the incarnate God who began God's saving work in creation.

5. In the story, Vince realized that Christ visited the lives of people around him through his actions. As family members, seek to discover ways that Christ works through you.

4

THE FEAST OF THE HOLY INNOCENTS

—

December 28

Today we turn to a theme that feels as gloomy as the winter nights that accompany us through these twelve days. The Feast of the Holy Innocents is the Good Friday of the Christmas season. Both remember death and call it a celebration: the *Feast* of the Innocents, *Good* Friday.

And what is there to celebrate on this day? This is the day on which we remember the death of the innocent children, which was ordered by King Herod as he attempted to kill the newborn Savior. This is the day on which we hear the story of Jesus and his family fleeing from the violence of Herod. This is the part of the Christmas narrative that is often forgotten. Here in the middle of the good news of the birth of the Messiah, we find a stark reminder of the reality of death. Even when God came into the world, death remained a reality. God did not take death away from the innocent children of Bethlehem, nor did Jesus take away his own death. He accepted both.

Therein lie the mystery and the revelation of this day: God did not come into the world to change how it was created, with both light and obscurity, life and death. God did come to redeem and to forgive the pain and hurt that obscurity and death cause. As creatures of this God of the cradle and cross, we are called to remember that we are capable still of slaughtering the innocent in all parts of creation. We are called to submit, as God did, to the laws of creation. We are called to walk as children of the light amidst the shadows.

SCRIPTURE

Matthew 2:13–16

Now after the wise men had left, an angel of God appeared to Joseph in a dream and said, "Get up, take the child and his mother, and flee to Egypt, and remain there until I tell you; for Herod is about to search for the child, to destroy him." Then Joseph got up, took the child and his mother by night, and went to Egypt, and remained there until the death of Herod. This was to fulfill what had been spoken by God through the prophet, "Out of Egypt I have called my son."

When Herod saw that he had been tricked by the wise men, he was infuriated, and he sent and killed all the children in and around Bethlehem who were two years old or under, according to the time that he had learned from the wise men.

THE PAGEANT

I started praying for snow on Thanksgiving day in my thirteenth year. The brown grass and leafless trees of November seemed to make me especially vulnerable to the icy seasonal winds. I longed for the soft, cold days of playing outside in the snow. A blanket of snow would warm up the world a bit.

The Thanksgiving turkey was carved that year by my only uncle, my mother's brother John. As he stood at the end of the smooth mahogany table in the dining room of the house I shared with my mother and two sisters, he made an announcement that would change life in that little house for the next several years: "You children are all going to have to get used to sharing this house. Grandmother is going to live with you for a while."

I think that my sisters were thrilled. My mother, who acted casual throughout this announcement, added, "I expect you all to treat her like a permanent member of our family." Mother pointed to me and added, "She will take the front bedroom, and you, Mark, can sleep on the pullout couch."

I was a little afraid of this grandmother. My other one talked with me and was always ready to laugh. This one always seemed to be slightly worried about something. I could never figure out what it might be. She seemed gentle and loving with my mother, but I always felt that I made her uneasy. Now she was going to live in my house and in my room. I wanted to run to that room and skip the Thanksgiving dinner. I thought I should show some sign of agreement or welcome, but I simply sat and ate. When I realized that my mother was still looking at me, I nodded my head in surrender.

Snow came on the following Sunday. It came in the big flakes that gather in warm-weather snowfalls, each flake almost defying gravity as it floats slowly to rest. When the snow fell that year, my spirits lifted. The world seemed so perfect under snow. A world bright, clean, and soft. A world that invited a playful slide or a face full of snow.

Grandmother came that day, too. I hoped it would be all right. I now would sleep in the living room. I was keenly aware that this was the room of the Christmas tree. This was the room of the newly acquired television set. This was the center of our family activity. Now I would call that center my own.

We all helped her carry her things into the front bedroom. She didn't really have much: a lamp, two suitcases, some hanging clothes, and a box of small things.

The crèche came out of that box. After she was settled into her room, she came out with the box and stated, "This has always been the sign of the approach of Christmas for me. I'll set it on this table by the window," she said as she carefully unwrapped painted porcelain figures. "When we put up the tree, this will be close to it. This will remind us of the meaning of the season."

"Do you have animal figurines, too?" I asked her. I remembered the animals in the scene that was displayed on the church lawn.

"The donkey comes from Italy," she whispered as she unfolded the wrapping from a pinkish-brown china donkey. "My sister Florence hand-delivered this to me when she returned from her once-in-a-lifetime trip to Europe."

She stopped unpacking and watched the snow fall for a few minutes. Turning back to her task, she said, "I am the last of my generation. So little of my world is left. These small things are large in memory."

The nativity scene took form on the table: angels on the roof of a porcelain stable, shepherds and stable animals, the holy family.

The small arrangement of statues became a focus for me as I waited the long child-weeks until Christmas. Throughout the day, when I was home I would admire the crèche from a close but safe distance.

On the first Monday morning, long before the house awoke, the stable came to life. I woke when the night was giving way to the soft light that carries the morning. I looked at the little cell of Middle Eastern life which had been set on the table in the corner by the window. I walked over and sat on the floor, cradling my chin on my arms, which were folded on the top of the table.

I squinted and tried to imagine what this had looked like in life. I imagined the figures moving. I wanted to talk to them. Still squinting, I reached up and moved one of the shepherds over to the manger. He knew that he was looking at the Messiah. He had been told so by an angel. I wondered if it was one of the angels who were on the roof of the stable. I moved him back into precisely the same spot where Grandma placed him. I paced Joseph up and down in front of the stable. Never having had a father that I remembered, I had to borrow from a fifties' version of new fathers which I had seen on television. They were always nervous and pacing. At the first sound of life from the bedrooms, I returned this stable to its proper inanimate form.

This went on every morning for the next few weeks. No one had told me not to touch these figures. It was just obvious from the way that Grandma handled them. No one touched them. So I kept my little Christmas pageants to myself.

As the season progressed, the play took on a form. First the shepherds would visit the manger, then the animals. Mary would sometimes go to the back of the stable and rest. While she did this, Joseph would stand straight behind the manger and watch over the Christchild. Sometimes the animals would just run back and forth in glee. The cow would run, a goat would jump, and the donkey had a kind of gallop that he and I developed together. Each dawn of that Advent season arrived to a reenactment of the silent night. That is what I called the play, "The Silent Night." And I was silent as I played. The silence of reverence for this sacred event. The silence of fear of being caught playing with the precious pieces of Grandma's life.

I suppose that it was inevitable. It happened two days before Christmas. The donkey just flew from his gallop into a wide arch toward the floor. As I reached to catch him, I saw him land in two pieces. His legs and tail were separated from the rest of his body. I couldn't touch him for a while. I was numb. I tried to think of some reason for this. Minutes might have already passed when I heard footsteps from the bedrooms. Grasping both pieces, I thought that I might put them in my pillow while I thought.

It was Grandma. It was as if she knew. She walked up in front of me and stared. I was on the fold-out bed with my hands behind my back. There was nothing to do. There was no excuse to make. I just held out both parts of the donkey to her. She stepped toward me and took the donkey from me by cupping her hands over mine.

I left the broken animal in her hands and threw my arms around her neck. "I've ruined a perfect Christmas. The whole scene was so right. Now it will always be flawed." She wrapped her arms around me.

On the third breath between tears, the word "sorry" made it out. As we talked, we just held still in this comfort embrace. She smelled a little like my mother but with the sharpness of age. As she held me, arms wrapped around my shoulders, I could see the tail piece of the donkey being held close to my eyes.

"Christmas is supposed to be perfect," I whispered as I started to move away from her. Her embrace felt good, but I felt so bad that I just wanted to throw myself into the familiar smell of my pillow.

She didn't let me go. She just spoke, her voice soft and clear. "No, Mark. Christmas is not supposed to be perfect. Christmas is supposed to be human. God entered this world, with all of its cracks and flaws. All of these pieces will break one day, just as all of the animals and people at that manger in Bethlehem came to their end. The Christmas event was a perfect God entering an imperfect world. This holy birth did not make the world perfect, it made it acceptable to God. We are not perfect, we are for-given. And so are you."

The donkey stands in my living room each Christmas, a cracked witness to the miracle of Christmas.

THE TRADITION

The Feast of the Holy Innocents comes at the end of three days that commemorate those who gave their lives so that the light of Christ might be shared with the world: Saint Stephen, who in will and deed became a martyr in the first century; Saint John the evangelist, who was willing to die for the cause of Christ but escaped death miraculously; and the innocent children whom Herod slew, and who became martyrs in deed but not in will. This feast has been commemorated since the fourth century as a day to honor innocents of all ages and times.

Who were the innocents? The story in the Gospel of Matthew identifies male children under the age of two as those slaughtered by Herod's soldiers. Herod believed he was deluded by the Magi and decided there would be no rival to his throne. This was not his first atrocity. Herod killed thousands of innocent people whom he suspected of plotting against him, including his wife, his mother-in-law, and his three sons. The number of the holy innocents has ranged from 14,000 in the early churches to 144,000 in medieval times. Modern writers, recognizing Bethlehem as a small Judean town, believe the number was 15 to 20 children.

One of the liturgies for this day speaks of the innocents as "buds of martyrs killed by the frost of hate as soon as they appeared."[1] It calls to mind other "innocents," such as the three hundred Lakota men, women, and children who on December

29, 1890, were slaughtered when four Hotchkiss guns opened up on an Indian camp at Wounded Knee, South Dakota. Women and children ran out of their teepees to seek the shelter of the ravine. The guns followed them to the ravine. After the massacre, bodies were found more than two miles away from the campsite. Survivors were rounded up in wagons and taken in a blizzard to the Pine Ridge army base. There was no room for these wounded people in the barracks, so the church was opened up. The people crawled out and entered God's house under the banner "Peace on Earth. Good will to all."

How does one observe the slaughter of innocents? The stories are told, the atrocities are remembered and not discounted. In early times, there was a tradition of setting aside this day to remember children and to hold Christmas parties for them. The festival was known as *Childermas*. In Germany, one custom called for a reenactment of the massacre in the form of a small whipping. Children would go about the streets with switches and boughs of green, demanding coins or little gifts. In Belgium, children would take possession of all the keys in their homes and lock unsuspecting adults in a closet or room. Freedom was restored only when an orange, a toy, money, or sweets were given as ransom.

For churches, Innocents' Day commemorated all newly baptized infants, thereby linking Christmas to the Easter mysteries of death and new life. The day was set aside as one to name and mourn all the innocent deaths of the previous year.

In the season of celebrating the light of the world, this day recognizes the gloom that Jesus entered. It stands as a reminder that God did not come to change or conquer the world but to forgive it. In the words of Saint John the evangelist, "If we say that we have no sin, we deceive ourselves. . . . If we confess our sins, then God who is faithful and just will forgive us our sins and cleanse us from everything that is wrong" (1 John 1:8–9).

ENTERING THE STORY: IDEAS FOR FAMILY CELEBRATION

As families, we do not often deal with the painful side of life. This is the gift and opportunity of this day, a day to recognize that God came not to change the world but to embrace it. Here are a few ideas for exploring this wonderful reality of Christmas.

1. After the evening meal, gather as a family by the Christmas tree. Give each person a small candle. Place a burning candle nearby. Take a moment for reflecting on personal imperfections. With a gentle spirit, give each person a moment to share his or her own reflection. As each is shared, allow the group to acknowledge those imperfections. When each person has finished his or her story, let others in the group individually share a word of acceptance or forgiveness. At the conclusion of this acceptance, each individual lights a candle from the central candle. When all candles have been lit, sing a favorite Christmas carol.

2. Take a walk outside on this wintry day. Appreciate the gift of this silent season and the beauty of the earth. Remember the gifts the earth gives to humankind, but go deeper into the thought of winter and remember it is a time of survival. On your walk, notice places where the earth is struggling to survive: a wounded tree, a polluted waterway, an abandoned farm. Bend over to touch the earth. Tell the earth you are sorry for the degradation humans bring upon it at times. Offer a prayer.

3. As the festivities of the Christmas season continue, join Flemish families and play a game of Christmas ransom. Children should be on the lookout for opportunities to capture unsuspecting adults in a room, closet, or small space. Do not let the adults out until they have given or promised a ransom of fruit, a small toy, sweets, or coins.

4. When remembering the story of the slaughter of the innocents, people of earlier times needed to make amends by honoring their children with a Christmas party. The festival was known as *Kindermas* in Germany. On this day, plan to spend as much of the day as possible with your children. Play their favorite games, cook a favorite meal, and take the time to tell each one of them why he or she is important to you.

5. At any given time, we are aware of places on the earth that are affected by war and tumult. Take a moment as a family and discuss the places that are affected during this Christmas season. Then, together offer a prayer for the innocents who are suffering. You may, as a family, choose to give a Christmas gift to a relief agency such as Catholic Relief Services, Lutheran World Relief, UNICEF, or Bread for the World.

5

The Song of Simeon

—

December 29

The angels proclaimed it on the night of Jesus' birth. Simeon announced it in the women's court of the Jerusalem Temple. God testified to its fulfillment in a Nazarene synagogue: "Peace on earth."

This peace brought forth freedom. It quieted fearful shepherds. It allowed a holy man, who waited his entire life for the Savior to come, to rest in peace. It brought a freedom and a new covenant to an oppressed nation and extended that new relationship with God to the entire world.

On the fifth day of Christmas, we sing with Simeon a psalm that celebrates the lifting of burdens and the transition to freedom in God's care: from waiting to receiving, from promises made to promises kept, from captivity to freedom. God's Word has been fulfilled.

SCRIPTURE

Luke 2:25–32

Now there was a man in Jerusalem whose name was Simeon; this man was righteous and devout, looking forward to the consolation of Israel, and the Holy Spirit rested on him. It had been revealed to him by the Holy Spirit that he would not see death before he had seen God's Messiah. Guided by the Spirit, Simeon came into the temple; and when the parents brought in the child Jesus, to do for him what was customary under the law, Simeon took him in his arms and praised God, saying,

"God, now you are dismissing your servant in peace, according to your word; for my eyes have seen your salvation, which you have prepared in the presence of all peoples, a light for revelation to the Gentiles and for glory to your people Israel."

OUT OF THE KENNEL

Sam awakened to barking. There was a high-pitched yapping, a middle-range bark, and a new sound this morning—a frenzied snorting noise. Sam woke up to barking every day, so he did what he always did: He stood up, stretched, yawned, and passed through the rubber doorway to his outside run. It was called a run but it was one small cage in a line of outside cages connected to the shelter. Sam had not really run for the two years that he had been at the shelter. All the running in Sam's life consisted of short bursts on a leash connected to a volunteer.

Life was pretty good for him otherwise. He had deep brown Labrador eyes, which had endeared him to the staff from the moment he arrived. A police officer had found him on a freeway dodging Thanksgiving day traffic. His black fur was ragged when the officer carried him in, wet, cold, and hungry. The worker on duty took one look at the yearling pup looking up at her and said, "That's one sad Sam you got there, Officer."

The name stuck. Sad Sam took well to life in the shelter. He was quiet but friendly. At least to the workers. When potential owners came by his kennel, he just looked at them quietly. No tail-wagging, no paws on the cage, no huffing and puffing, eagerly convincing them to take him home. When strangers walked through the kennels, he would go to his pad, lie down, and watch them pass. One man was looking for a watch dog and said, "That one would never do." Most were looking for puppies. Even at Sam's young age, he was beyond the cuddly puppy stage.

Sometime in the middle of his first year, someone began to let him wander within the shelter during the day. He was perfect for the job. He was never aggressive with the other animals, neither dogs nor cats. He greeted everyone who entered the front door but never demanded attention. He knew how to just be there—everyone's buddy. Sometime during that first year, someone changed his name from "Sad Sam" to "Good Neighbor Sam."

One year passed, then another. It looked as if Sam was to be a permanent resident of the shelter. The routine was the same every day. Wake up, take a nap out in the run, come back to the inside cage for the daily feeding, hide your head in the corner when they mopped the floors with the disinfectant because it burned the nose, and then wait for the best part—the release to become "Good Neighbor Sam, the Shelter Dog."

It wasn't all fun. Sam had a part of his ear missing from a German shepherd who came into the shelter. He always worked to stay away from cats. They were so resistant to his friendship. He tired of the constant barking in the kennel. The worst thing was the front door. He tried to slip out once in the first year. He made it out but did not get back in for three days. January temperatures nibbled off the edge of his other ear. He was cold, tired, and hungry when the mail carrier returned him to the shelter. It had not been worth it. Sam stayed away from the front door. It was Sam's rule.

In the afternoon, it was walk time. A couple of volunteers came to walk the dogs. They would go from cage to cage, red nylon leashes in hand, and give each dog a short walk. Sam would follow them as they progressed, making sure that he was not forgotten. The walk was never long enough or fast enough for Sam. As they traveled away from the shelter, he would run, head high, pulling against the strap. On the return trip, he stopped and sniffed every possible place of interest until his volunteer would pull and coax him into a speedier trip home.

The shelter was home to Sam. He had seen new dogs come and go constantly in the kennels on each side of him. No dog had been there longer than he. He had no specific worker whom he was loyal to; he liked them all. This was his place. He owned it by occupancy.

Then one day some strangers stopped at his kennel and asked the attendant, "This one is how old you say?"

"That's Good Neighbor Sam," the worker responded. "He must be about three years old. He was pretty much still a pup when he came here around two years ago. He's real friendly and easygoing. Needs to be somewhere in the country or something, though. He's got a reputation for getting lost in the city."

Within moments, Sam was hooked to a new blue leash and led to a pickup truck. They put him on the front seat between them. It was nice. The little girl didn't stop scratching him behind his ears until the truck stopped about an hour later. They led him into a house—no barking, no disinfectant, no kennels. Sam was feeling strange about it all when they set a plate of canned dog food in front of him. He didn't know it was canned dog food. He didn't even know it was dog food. It wasn't really even time to eat. It was late afternoon. But Sam, being a good neighbor and a dog after all, ate the whole pile of food in just a few gulps. He chased the plate around the floor for a while with his tongue, licking the last fragments of this new delicacy from the plate.

"Time for bed, Sammy," the little girl said as she motioned for him to follow. He went as far as her bedroom door then turned around. He needed a kennel. That was the rule. At night you sleep alone in a kennel. He found an end table at the far end of the living room couch and slithered under it, head first, looking for confinement.

"Just let him be," the man said as he turned out the lights. "He'll get used to things around here."

Sammy (for that seemed to be his new name) liked things in this new place. He ate twice a day now and that was easy to get used to. He slept under the end table, and he had almost constant attention from his new people. He was adjusting to most things well. The one problem centered around the front door. He stayed away from it: Sam's rule. These people just opened the door and called him outside—no leash, no volunteer. He knew better. He needed a leash. He stood his ground until they would get the blue leash and take him outside. This went on for two days until the girl had him outside one day. She knelt beside him, unclasped the leash, and said "Run, Sammy. There is a whole farm for you to run on. Run around and enjoy yourself."

Sam stayed close to her.

She said it again. "Run, Sammy." Then she ran. Sam ran beside her. They ran to the edge of a large pasture, then the girl stopped.

Sam didn't. No leash, no freeways. Nothing stopping him. No rules. He ran through the smell of green grass. He jumped at some birds as they flew from the ground before him. He ran until he came to a grove of trees and stopped because he wanted to. He now understood life without the leash.

Then Sam turned around. He ran back to his new home.

THE TRADITION

Three psalms grace the infancy narratives in Luke's gospel: a mother's acceptance of God's will (*Magnificat*, Luke 1:46–55), a father's prayer of thanksgiving (*Benedictus*, Luke 1:68–79), and a holy one's prayer of confidence (*Nunc Dimittus*, Luke 2:29–32). Each psalm tells the story of God's promise of salvation to those who are of low degree, to those who walk in shadows, and to those awaiting the glory of Israel. Each psalm promises a freedom from the burdens each carried: For Mary, it was a freedom from social oppression. The lowly were to be exalted and remembered. For Zechariah, it was a freedom from fears of no progeny, lack of safety, and the gloom of death. For Simeon, it was the freedom from years of longing and the oppression of unfulfilled dreams.

Since the early centuries of Christianity, the psalms have been included in the liturgy of the hours—those sacred times designated to honoring the rhythm and tone of a day's passing. The *Benedictus*, Zechariah's prayer of thanksgiving at the birth of his son John, is said at dawn. It prepares our way for the beginning of a new day in God's creation.

Mary's canticle, the *Magnificat*, is sung during evening prayer (Vespers). As dusk descends upon the earth, the words of the mother of God proclaim a message of God's continuing presence and care to the children of God. God upholds the humble and blesses those who fear the Almighty.

The Song of Simeon is recited at the close of the day (Compline). As the shadows of the night cover the earth, Simeon's proclamation of a light of revelation to all people of the earth is a beacon of hope that carries us through the night. It is also prayed as someone is dying, sharing the peace of Simeon as he or she departs from this world. "Now, Master, you can let your servant go in peace."

Those words of peace, however, are not merely the quieting prayers of a humble follower of God. They were words spoken when slaves were emancipated in the ancient Middle East. They were words of freedom, claiming release from bondage. When Simeon chose those words, he spoke to the bondage in which he had been enslaved: awaiting the fulfillment of the covenant, God's two-thousand-year-old promise of salvation. Simeon had been in bondage to a deep yearning to see God in his lifetime, as were generations of Israelites.

When Simeon saw the child Jesus in the Temple, he knew the promise had been fulfilled. The child would free not only the Israelites but all of humankind from the bondage of false expectations and promises, from the burden of trying to be perfect in God's sight, from the heavy load of sin and guilt.

One thousand years after Christ's birth, another servant of God proclaimed a message of liberty to God's people, this time from civil authority. Thomas à Becket was the archbishop of Canterbury. He struggled with the king of England, Henry II, about the authority of the crown over that of the church. During evening vespers on December 29, 1171, Thomas's foes descended upon him and killed him for his resistance to the power of the king.

To honor Thomas à Becket and the role he played in upholding the freedom of God's people, keys are collected from every door, drawer, coffer, and cupboard in the house and sent with a child to the church for a blessing. Though Thomas's life was lost, he, like Simeon, departed in peace. Another custom celebrating freedom from captivity is to scatter bread crumbs and bacon rind for the sparrows or other birds on this day.

The doors to freedom were opened that day in the women's court when Mary and Joseph came to present Jesus to God. What they did not realize was that God had presented Jesus that day to the whole world. The door had been opened to the world. The Word became flesh and dwelt among us.

ENTERING THE RITUAL: IDEAS FOR FAMILY CELEBRATION

In the Christmas story, we often forget the oppression that the holy family and the people of Israel experienced. We focus on the comfort and quiet of the manger with attending shepherds and angels, and forget the walk toward freedom that only Christ's death would bring. On this day of the Christmas season, we uphold God's gift of freedom.

1. Say the *Benedictus* (Luke 1:68–79) at dawn, the *Magnificat* (Luke 1:46–55) at dusk, and the Song of Simeon (Luke 2:29–32) at the close of the day.

2. In many cultures, birds and their ability to fly are a symbol of freedom. During the day, go outside in your yard or to a nearly park and scatter bread crumbs and/or bacon rind for winter birds.

3. Locks and keys are necessary for safety in today's world. If you have children, have them gather the keys your family uses. Say a prayer that these keys may continue to protect you but not prevent you from doing God's work in the world.

4. Look back over the last year and remember times when each family member needed forgiveness. Celebrate the freedom of the words "I'm sorry" and "I forgive you."

5. As a family, name and discuss the people you know whose freedom is limited: those who are disabled socially, mentally, economically, emotionally, or physically. Choose one and decide together how you can work toward helping her or him gain more freedom.

6

THE WOMEN OF CHRISTMAS

December 30

In the beginning, the Word of God scattered the shadows of the void and created life and light. In the recesses of a virgin's womb, that Word became flesh and created new hope for God's creation.

The blessings of the incarnation, both those given and those received by three women, are at the center of celebration on this day of the Christmas season. Anna, a widowed prophetess, and Elizabeth, a once-infertile women, serve as midwives to the birth of God's Word in the world. They, along with Mary, the mother of God, are bearers and interpreter's of a divine event: God the Creator had acted again in renewing creation.

On this day of the twelve, we recognize the role of women in giving life to the world: the life of renewed hope, the life of remembered promises, the life of enduring faith, the life of new purpose.

SCRIPTURE

Luke 2:36–38

There was also a prophet, Anna the daughter of Phanuel, of the tribe of Asher. She was of a great age, having lived with her husband seven years after her marriage, then as a widow to the age of eighty-four. She never left the temple but worshiped there with fasting and prayer night and day. At that moment she came, and began to praise God and to speak about the child to all who were looking for the redemption of Jerusalem.

ONLY WEEDS

Rosamund was fetching water. She did not like to carry water. When she carried it with her arms outstretched, an equally filled pail on either side, her arms would ache. When she carried it with her arms hanging down, the pails bumped her legs and the water spilled out. Mama's last words when she left for the well were, "Like a bird Rosa, keep your arms out like a bird." Rosamund set the pails down and wondered if wings ever ached.

She heard the sound of horses coming up the road. She stepped aside to let a carriage go by. The carriage driver looked straight ahead. He had no passengers. The carriage was filled with flowers: bright yellow gladiolas, pink orchids, vines of deep violet bougainvillea, and the sweet perfume of jasmine. She had never seen so many flowers out of a garden at the same time. The carriage was like a vase with wheels. She could still see it when it reached the center of the village. He stopped at the church and started to carry in flowers. Rosa wondered who had died. Usually she would have heard about it. The village was small that way.

As he came out for his third load of flowers, Rosa dared to ask, "Pardon me, Sir, has there been a death?" He turned and looked at her with amazement. "Have you forgotten, young girl, that this is *Posadas,* the preparation for Christmas? These flowers are gifts for the Christchild. You, too, should bring something lovely for the Christchild."

Rosa responded without even thinking, "But I have nothing to give."

Rosa felt as if someone had put a stone on her shoulders. She turned and headed home. "How can I give something when I have nothing?" she wondered. "Maybe I could find some flour or lentils in the cupboard, but they would be nothing next to all of those wonderful flowers."

At home she sat quietly through supper. She didn't want to tell anyone why she felt so bad. She was afraid they would join her in sorrow. They, too, had nothing to give. No, she would carry this stone alone.

As she went to bed, the night seemed gloomier than usual. She knelt and prayed a simple prayer: "Dear God, tell me how. How can I give? What can I give?"

Morning came. Rosa hung her head. She wanted to give a gift of her own. Her family had no flowers. They had nothing beautiful to give. What would she do?

After breakfast, she decided to walk into the village and look at all the flowers that had been delivered the day before. Maybe she would think of something on the walk.

Rosamund loved the walk to the village. It was just over a little hill from her home. When she reached the top of the hill, she would look down on the village and imagine what all the people were doing in their houses. As she reached the top of the hill that day, she was surrounded by bright light. An angel was in the light. She covered her eyes and turned to run home.

"Do not run home, Rosa," the angel commanded. "You have a great gift to deliver to the church for the Christmas mass."

Rosa turned to face the angel, her eyes cast downward. "I own nothing of beauty and have nothing to give," she whispered.

"Take these plants from along the path, gather them into pots, and bring them to the church. They will be your gift," the angel directed.

Rosa looked up at the angel, "But these plants are just green weeds. They would look silly next to all of the flowers in church."

The bright light faded. She was alone.

Rosamund did as she was instructed. She went back home to get pots for the plants and a little wagon. She took the plants to the church as the sun was going down. She didn't want anyone to see her bringing weeds to the Christmas festival. She lined the twelve pots along the front of the church, down a few steps from the other flowers on the altar. She tiptoed out the side door and hoped that no one had seen her. In two days it would be Christmas, and no one would know who had brought them.

The two days passed slowly. All Rosamund did was worry. She worried that she had misunderstood the angel. She worried that maybe she hadn't really seen an angel at all. She worried that everyone would be upset with a church full of weeds.

Christmas Day came. She walked the path with her family to the Christmas mass. As they approached the church, she heard the murmurs.

They were all looking at her. She was sick at heart. Someone must have seen her with the weeds. She had disgraced herself and her family. Then the priest came out the front door.

"Rosa, you are finally here. Tell us where you got the most beautiful flowers of the season. I saw you deliver them. They are so festive."

Rosa was confused. She stepped past the priest and looked into the church. Her green weeds had become the brightest, most beautiful red flowers she had ever seen.

She joined the crowd as they entered the church. The front of the church glowed with red. In the fiery glow, she saw him in the front row. He was on his knees. There knelt her angel. As she passed, he whispered, "These plants were a special gift to you from God. When you gave them away, they became the poinsettia, the Christmas plant. You blessed this Christmas mass with your gift. God blessed your giving."[1]

THE TRADITION

The birth of a child heralds the promise of a new beginning and hope. It was no less a proclamation for the child Jesus, but much more. The birth of Jesus brought forward a two-thousand-year-old promise of hope. It was a blessing of birth and renewal for the entire planet, for all the creatures of the earth, and three women professed this understanding of the incarnation.

Elizabeth, the elderly wife of a priest, was the first to experience the God of the incarnation. God brought new life to the family of Elizabeth and Zechariah when she become pregnant after many years of infertility. When Mary, her young cousin, came to visit her, the child within Elizabeth's womb leapt with joy. The Holy Spirit filled Elizabeth with words of blessing for the woman who bore the Child of God and for the Savior himself. Elizabeth proclaimed, "Blessed are you among women and blessed is the fruit of your womb" (Luke 1:42).

In response to Elizabeth's announcement, Mary blessed God. She praised God for remembering God's humble follower. Then she extended the blessings beyond herself: "God has brought down the powerful from their thrones and lifted up the lowly. God has filled the hungry with good things and sent the rich away empty. God has helped . . . Israel in remembrance of God's mercy" (Luke 1:52–54). Mary blessed God for all the wondrous deeds birthed upon the community of God's creation since the time of Abraham.

Cyril of Alexandria, a fifth-century theologian, wrote a sermon about Mary's prayer: "Thanks to you the heavens rejoice, the angels and archangels keep festival. . . . Thanks to you the whole creation . . . came to the knowledge of the truth. Thanks to you . . . the whole world therefore rejoices."[2] God's light was shed on the whole world and salvation brought to all peoples.

Anna, a Jewish prophet, proclaimed that very message to the bystanders when Mary and Joseph brought Jesus to be presented to God in the Temple. Anna had seen Mary ascending the uncovered gateway leading into the Court of the Women. Anna praised God's name. She then turned to those gathered and spoke about the child to all those who looked forward to the deliverance of Jerusalem.

Each woman graced the world with a proclamation of hope: The Messiah had been born.

On this day, the sixth day of Christmas, an old British church tradition recalled the journey of Mary and the blessings that new birth brings to each family. Women who gave birth during the previous year met at the entrance of the church to receive the blessing of the people of God. They were given a lighted candle in the narthex and were sprinkled with blessed water: a sign of the waters of birth and baptism. A psalm of thanksgiving was recited. The women and their children then followed the minister to the altar. Standing in the presence of

God, a prayer of petition was offered that the mother and offspring would know the joys of everlasting life.

For centuries, women have proclaimed mercy and comfort, nurture and life-giving peace. In each era and culture, the role of women changes, but the strength of their proclamation continues. The blessings and the hope of the women of Christmas are important for our era and culture. Whatever pathway a woman chooses to follow, her calling in Christ is the proclamation and blessing of Christ's presence in the world. Through the incarnation, God cradled creation in the womb of God's Word and brought forth mercy and comfort to all peoples of the earth—indeed, to all of creation.

ENTERING THE RITUAL: IDEAS FOR FAMILY CELEBRATION

The blessing of women and their children is an affirmation of the traditional role of women as bearers of life. In many cultures, both ancient and modern, the role of women as bearers and sustainers of life was extended to their communities and their churches. They were the keepers of faith and life. Today, this life-giving role takes many other shapes as women extend their care to all aspects of society and creation itself.

1. Recognize the life-giving nature of shared recreation. During this holiday season, plan a family vacation. This vacation can be taken during the holiday season or sometime over the next year. Focus on the renewing aspects of rest and "re-creation."

2. When your family gathers (for a meal or evening prayer), discover together a life-giving quality in each family member (for example, laughter, meal preparation, taking care of pets, creative thinking). Pray together a thanksgiving prayer for God's life-giving gift to and in each individual.

3. Prepare and serve a special meal for the women in your family (grandmothers, mothers, daughters, close friends). Allow each woman to share a dream for themselves and their family.

4. Gather the women in your life, both friends and family, in a sacred circle in your living room. Light a candle and place it on a coffee table in the middle of your circle. Remember the lives and witness of the women of Christmas: Mary, whose life was full of joy and sorrow; Anna, whose name means "grace" and who announced God's gift to bystanders in the Temple; and Elizabeth, for whom the Word of God was all-powerful. Go around the circle and give each woman the opportunity to share wisdom, talk about a time of sorrow, or tell the story of God's work in her life.

5. God entered the world as a human through a human mother. God placed humans in the world using the earth as mother. List the qualities of being a mother. What do mothers do? Then, whether you are sitting cozily around a winter fire, riding in the car, or hiking in a park or in your neighborhood, determine together how the earth mothers us.

7

THE FEAST OF THE HOLY FAMILY

—

December 31

At the stable in Bethlehem, God placed God's Child in the hands of a carpenter and a young maiden. God's Child joined a family—the holy family. We often think of it as the perfect family, but it was not. This family began their life together amidst doubt and possibly even scandal. Yet God chose this family to join. In joining a family, God became part of the human community. God became a member of our family. And we became a member of God's community.

God entered into a very intimate relationship with creation through this act. Jesus walked with, listened to, struggled with, celebrated and cried with the family he chose.

He experienced a very human institution: a family.

On the Sunday within the octave of Christmas, the Feast of the Holy Family is observed. Because it is a movable feast, we have chosen to celebrate it on this day. It is a time to remember the holy family. It is a time to celebrate the institution of family in its many forms.

SCRIPTURE

Luke 2:42–52

When he was twelve years old, they went up as usual for the festival. When the festival was ended and they started to return, the boy Jesus stayed behind in Jerusalem, but his parents did not know it. Assuming that he was in the group of travelers, they went a day's journey. Then they started to look for him among their relatives and friends. When they did not find him, they returned to Jerusalem to search for him.

After three days they found him in the temple, sitting among the teachers, listening to them, and asking them questions. And all who heard him were amazed at his understanding and his answers. When his parents saw him they were astonished; and his mother said to him, "Child, why have you treated us like this? Look, your father and I have been searching for you in great anxiety."

He said to them, "Why were you searching for me? Did you not know that I must be in my Father's house?" But they did not understand what he said to them.

Then he went down with them and came to Nazareth, and was obedient to them. His mother treasured all these things in her heart. And Jesus increased in wisdom and in years, and in divine and human favor.

THE WHOLE FAMILY

Hal balanced the sack of Christmas packages against the back car door, using his knee to prop them up while he unlocked the car. His son Eric, eight years old and on his first real Christmas shopping trip with his dad, sat down, more tired than he could remember ever being.

"Have we got all of the presents we need, Dad?" he asked in a tone that sounded more like a lament than a question.

"Just about, Eric," Hal replied. "We still have to get one for your Uncle Rob." He drove slowly through the busy parking lot. "I thought we could find him something at that sport shop that's on our way home."

"You know he's not really my uncle, Dad," Eric said, hoping to skip this last stop. "I don't really get it. At one moment, you talk about having just one sister, my Aunt Sue. Then the next day, you talk about Uncle Phil, Uncle Richard, Uncle Jim, and Uncle David. And a bunch of aunts, too. If you have just one sister, how can all of these other people be family?"

Hal pulled up in front of the sports shop, shut the car off, and answered his son. "They are family, Eric. We just were not born as family. We grew together as our lives progressed."

Hal restarted the car to get the heater running again as he continued. "The first time I saw your Uncle Phil, he wasn't anybody's uncle. My family, the first one—Mom, Dad, and my sister Sue—had just moved to a new community. We couldn't find a house, so we rented a summer cottage on a nearby lake. I thought it would be fantastic. I figured that I would fish and swim all day long. I hadn't counted on one thing—being alone. Dad went to work, Mom did housework and had coffee with some new neighbors, and my sister was too young to count for much. So I sat, bored.

"Sometimes I fished off the end of the dock. The fishing there wasn't much good. In fact, the only time I caught fish was in the boat with my dad. But I sat on the dock and fished anyway. There was nothing else to do. I would watch the red and white bobber drift up and down with the waves and sometimes pretend that a fish was pulling it down. I'd jerk the rod back to set the hook in the fish and the whole thing—hook, weight, and bobber—would fly back past me toward the shore. Then I'd cast it out and sit again.

"It was from this dock that I first saw Uncle Phil. I'd heard that a mother and her five children would be coming to spend the summer. The children's father had died tragically in the spring. They were going to summer at a beloved family place and put their lives together."

"Was the mother Grandma Irene?" Eric asked, happy to be able to figure this out.

"You're right, Eric," Hal continued. "She's not your blood grandmother but she is family and she is a grandmother, so that's what we call her."

"Why don't you get back to the dock, Dad?" Eric coached.

Hal continued. "There were no kids on the little point where the cabins were located, so it was a very quiet place. As I sat that day, in silence, watching my bobber and hoping for it to go down, the silence was interrupted—not just a little but a lot. Five kids and their mother came out of the car with their mouths open. Chrissy and David, the youngest, were crying.

Susan and Greg, the oldest, were telling them to be quiet, and Phil, the one in the middle, was running along the beach, singing a dumb little song. He was about twelve years old and almost six feet tall, most of it legs. He had thick glasses and a haircut that drew a straight line just above his eyebrows. I'd been looking forward to having company, but now, in the face of reality, I wasn't so sure. Within minutes, Phil and Greg were on the dock with me, telling me why I wasn't catching fish. It sounds like brothers, doesn't it?

"That was the first day of a lifetime relationship. They were a family in need, and we were, too. We all had been displaced in one way or another. So we filled those needs with one another. Through the years, there have been very few important holidays or events that we haven't celebrated together, both the good ones and the hard ones."

Eric looked towards the store, ready to go inside. Almost as an afterthought, he asked, "What about the rest of the family? There are four names you haven't mentioned."

Hal smiled. "You mean Grandpa Bob and his kids. They came along a few years later. Bob was a friend of my dad's, and he lost his young wife to a sudden illness. He was left with four kids: another family with a hole to fill. My dad introduced him to Grandma Irene, and they joined their two families—officially. They got married. But the large family—the one we're a part of—continued. Through marriages, births, deaths, and long-distance moves. We are a real family. That will never change. So we'd better get going and get that gift for your Uncle Phil."

THE TRADITION

During the seventeenth century, devotion to the family of Jesus enjoyed widespread popularity. Christmas was seen not only as a time to recognize God's gift to the world in the humanity of Jesus Christ, but as a time to remember the family into which Jesus was born. It became a time to recognize the importance of the holy family in Jesus' upbringing.

The Christian tradition shares two gospel stories on the Feast of the Holy Family: the presentation of Jesus in the Temple by his parents when he was an infant, and the Passover journey to the Temple when Jesus was twelve years old. Mary and Joseph were present, guiding Jesus as any parents guide the life of their children.

Francis de Sales, a monk who lived during this time of great devotion to the holy family, understood the three persons of the holy family to be the earthly component of the heavenly Trinity. For Francis, Jesus was the center of the convergence of these spiritual triangles: Father, Son, and Holy Spirit; Jesus, Mary, and Joseph.

Another person associated with this day, December 31, was an early Christian holy man, Pope Sylvester. He lived in the fourth century and was part of the assembly of theologians and elders of the church who articulated the heavenly triangle of three persons in one God in the Nicene Creed. The tradition attached to Sylvester's feast day involves another union—that of a husband and wife. Sylvester Night was a time of oracle games to find out what the new year would bring. A devotional practice developed in some European countries, where girls recited rhymed prayers to ask for dreams that would reveal their future spouse.

In France and in French Canada, a custom came down from medieval times whereby a father would make the sign of the cross, the mark of the heavenly Trinity, on the foreheads of his wife and children. He would ask for God's blessing on his family for the coming year. In other parts of Europe, this blessing would occur at the stroke of midnight.

The blessings on New Year's Eve extend to the animal world in the Middle Eastern countries of Syria and Lebanon. On this night, families put out a bowl of water and a dish of wheat for camels. This act of kindness finds its roots in the legend of the youngest camel who carried the Magi to visit the holy family. The camel fell down exhausted from the long journey. The Christchild blessed the camel and conferred immortality on it.

In these cultures, it is the camel who bears Christmas gifts to children rather than Saint Nicholas.

The Feast of the Holy Family is celebrated within the twelve days of Christmas to draw attention to the family that received God in human form and to the importance of that family in nurturing and supporting God's Child.

ENTERING THE STORY: IDEAS FOR FAMILY CELEBRATION

The season of Christmas often provides time to focus on the family, as intimate family members, as groups of friends and neighbors, as extended family over time and distance. These activities provide a variety of opportunities to celebrate the ever-growing definitions of the family of God.

1. After the evening meal, have two members of your family read the appointed biblical stories for this day (the presentation of Jesus in the temple as an infant, Luke 2:22–40; and the boy Jesus in the Temple, Luke 2:42–52). Pause for a moment of reflection. Discuss how Jesus was a blessing to his family. Then have the elder of the house place the sign of the cross on the foreheads of each family member, blessing them for the coming year.

2. Celebrate the tradition of Saint Lucia Day on the Feast of the Holy Family. Saint Lucia Day is traditionally observed on December 13 as a family festival. Saint Lucia was a fourth-century woman who gave all her dowry to the poor. Thereafter, she was seen in many places where people needed help. To emulate Saint Lucia, the oldest daughter prepares coffee and buns, which she serves to other members of the family. She is normally dressed in a long white gown, and on her head she bears a crown of lighted candles. Follow the tradition or encourage all the children to prepare breakfast for their parents.

3. The Feast of the Holy Family falls within the octave of Christmas. Octaves were celebrated in the early church as a smaller, yet still significant, occasion honoring the feast day. In the spirit of Christmas, have your church or a group of neighbors contribute mittens and hats to a local women's shelter, and animal treats for

dogs and cats to the local animal shelter. Remember that Christmas is a day to celebrate all of creation—our nuclear, extended, and global families.

4. Go over your Christmas card list. Take turns telling stories of how friends and other relatives became part of your "family."

5. For the Christmas holidays, keep a notebook out and jot down different configurations of family as seen in novels (were Huckleberry Finn and Jim a family?), movies (were Snow White and the seven dwarfs a family?), and television programs. On the eve of the Epiphany, the twelfth night of the Christmas season, share the discoveries.

8

The Name of Jesus

January 1

Yahweh, God of Hosts; El Shaddai, God of the Mountains; El Elyon, Exalted One, Most High: These are names of God, names that set God over God's people. They are names to be both feared and respected.

Immanuel, God with us; Jesus, the One who saves: These are the names of the incarnate God, given by the community of angels, which set God among the people. They are names that draw people near, to be called upon and loved.

When Jesus was given his name, humankind's relationship with God changed. The God of mystery and divine distance became a God who walked among the people, who joined them in their journey on earth. From this point onward, we have been on a first-name basis with God.

On this first day of the new year, we celebrate the new name given to the God of the universe: the holy name of Jesus. We recognize the role of community in the giving of a name. And we remember that time itself was given a new name by Christians on Christmas Day: A.D., Anno Domini, in the year of God.

SCRIPTURE

Luke 2:21

After eight days had passed, it was time to circumcise the child; and he was called Jesus, the name given by the angel before he was conceived in the womb.

EELPOUT

"Johnson, Walter."

"Here."

"Hines, Peter."

"Here."

"Smith, Zachary."

"Here."

Graham listened and watched very closely as the roll was called. He listened to names that were new to him and connected them with faces he had never seen. This was his first day in a new school, and just knowing a few of the names of the strangers around him helped Graham to feel less alone.

"Parker, Graham."

He answered loudly, hoping someone would notice him, "Here."

No one did. It was as if he were invisible. All day long, people had been looking past him. Oh, not all people. The teachers went out of their way to introduce him to the classes. It almost made things worse. There he sat with the teacher talking about the nice new boy who would add so much to the class. He stared straight ahead, embarrassed at the attention. Yet there was no attention. The rest of the class stared straight ahead, too, as if the teacher were talking about the inventor of modern hydraulics or something like that. He felt alone. And he was alone—the only new kid in school.

One class wasn't like that: physical education. He stood in a line of seventh-grade boys, white shoes, white socks, white shorts, white T-shirts, and bare legs. The teacher gave him no special attention.

"Wilson, John."

Graham wondered why phys ed always did it that way: last name first. His name sounded different that way—more important maybe, less like himself.

Yablonski was the last to be called. Graham wondered what it would be like to have a name like that. He also wondered how any seventh-grader could be that big. This Yablonski kid was at least two inches taller than Graham's father. He seemed friendly enough. Maybe he would talk to Graham soon. Graham would remember his name. Somebody had to talk to him soon. If they didn't, he felt like he would not be able to stand coming back to this school.

After lunch, all of the boys went out to the east playground. Graham stood and watched as they played a game in which they all ran and slid down an icy hill. At the bottom of the hill, they would all pile on top of one another. As they would run and slide, they would yell, "Hog pile!" As they slid past, he tried to identify them: Wilson, Johnson, Hines, and Smith. He knew them all: John, Zachary, Peter, Walter. When Yablonski slid, everyone cleared the way at the bottom. Graham figured that they didn't want somebody as big as their dads landing on them. As they played, they shouted at each other.

"Hey, Weasel, I'm going to cream you this time."

"Pinto, you go first."

As Yablonski came sliding at high speed, they screamed. "Moose landing, get out of the way."

Graham watched awhile, then began to run and slide beside the other boys, but not quite with them. It wasn't long until he heard the warning, "Look out, Parker. I'm coming through." At the same time that the words hit his ears, a body hit the back of his legs. Hog pile. He was in the hog pile, and somebody knew his name.

Each day Graham felt more at home. He had friends now, especially Weasel and Moose. He hung around with a larger bunch of guys at lunch. This school didn't seem to be as hard as his last one. The new house was nice. He liked his room and the new family room. There was just one thing wrong: his name. They all called him Parker. That, of course, was his family name, but he wanted something better. He was the only one of his friends who didn't have a nickname. He didn't really feel like he fit without one.

He tried out some secretly. He thought of dangerous names like Ace or Sharky. They didn't really seem to fit him. He tried borrowing one from TV reruns like Goober or Rocky. He tried animal names like Bear or Cougar. He couldn't figure out how to get anyone to use whatever name he might pick. He tried once. He casually said, "Just call me Park," as they were walking to school. When they split up to go to their lockers at school, Weasel said, "See you later, Parker."

Graham figured out that somebody else had to give you a nickname. He wondered if anyone ever would.

Christmas vacation came. The boys spent each afternoon out on the lake by the south edge of town. Graham had never even walked on a frozen lake before, much less been ice fishing, but he learned fast. Moose had an auger for drilling holes. Each boy had a small rod that he used. Graham had to wait three days before he caught a fish. He watched each of the other boys catch at least one silver-brown walleye. They would all get excited, gather around the hole as the fish came up and then pay close attention to their own lines for a while afterwards, assured that there really were fish in the lake.

It was during one of these times of concentration that Graham felt a gentle tug at his line.

"Maybe it's just a perch," he thought because the touch was so light. The others had taught him what to do when he had a bite.

"Set the hook," Moose had told him. "Yank the rod straight up toward the sky. If the fish is big enough to be worth catching, he'll yank it back down."

Graham yanked. He felt like he was hooked up to a rock. It just didn't move.

"Snag," Weasel said. "You must be hooked to a log or something."

Then the log began to swim. Graham tried to pull against the fish a little bit, but it seem to him that this fish could swim anywhere it liked. The boys all gathered around the hole.

"This is a big one," Pinto said. "I'll bet that it's another ten-pound walleye like my Uncle Oscar caught up by the creamery."

"I'll bet it's a real trophy," Moose said. He called out to the others, "Come on over, we've got a real trophy hunter here."

It sounded good to Graham but first of all he had to get his trophy on the ice. He reeled in and reeled in until he could just about see the fish through the surface hole, and then the fish would swim away, taking the line back off of his reel. As he reeled, his buddies encouraged him. When the fish stripped line out, the mechanism of the reel caused a shrieking sound. The boys all groaned with it and started offering their condolences. But he hadn't lost the fish yet. He would get it. He knew.

Fifteen minutes went by. His hands were cold and tired. The fish seemed tired, too. Maybe this time Graham would get it to the surface and through the hole. Everyone gathered again around the hole. Weasel was ready to grab the fish. Graham reeled. He saw a huge black shadow beneath the hole. He was thrilled. This was the biggest fish he had ever seen. Then the boys started to groan.

"Burbot," Moose said.

"Mud blower."

"It's an Eelpout," Pinto said just as the fish flopped up on the ice.

This was the slimiest, ugliest fish that Graham had ever seen. He didn't even dare take it off the line. As he reached for the fish, it slipped off the hook and slithered over to the hole.

"Eelpout, Eelpout," the boys shouted.

Graham pushed the fish back in the hole with his feet and sat down to grieve this catch. There would be no trophy. There would be no glory story. Certainly no one would ever call him a trophy hunter again.

As the sun began to set, the boys started on their way home. Graham was the first to be dropped off as they walked. Just when he reached the steps, he heard it. It made the day worthwhile.

"See you tomorrow, Eelpout."

THE TRADITION

In many cultures, naming ceremonies were sacred events. Naming someone was part of creating an identity. Elders sought names for a newborn child through meditation, prayer, or dreaming. A person's name was an expression of the essential nature of its bearer. On the day of the naming ceremony, the child was held up and the name pronounced to the gathered community and to the universe.

The birth of any child is heralded by his or her parents with the pronouncement of a name. They may have found the name in a baby book or given it in honor of relatives or a famous person. As the child grows, new names can be added by the community of people that touch the child's life: a nickname from schoolmates, a name taken during religious ceremonies, a name change when someone is married.

Four names are associated with New Year's Day: the Roman god Janus; a Greek saint, Basil; Mary, the mother of God; and Jesus. Each name brings a story.

The Romans began the celebration of the beginning of the year on January 1 in 153 B.C.E. It was placed on the first month following the winter solstice. Janus was the Roman god of all beginnings. He had two faces—one looking back to the old year, the other looking forward. The festival honoring the new year, Calends, was a time of great festivity and widespread license.

As the merriment and frivolity of this day grew, the Roman church decided to add its mark by making January 1 a day of penitence and fasting. It was a time to close rifts and heal the disputes of the previous year. The secular tradition of making New Year's resolutions may have its roots in this ancient penitential observation.

The Eastern Orthodox church honors the life of Saint Basil, a fourth-century Greek bishop, on January 1. Basil's name is linked with the giving of wishes and blessings. On this day, many Greek families bake a New Year's cake called *Vasilopeta*, or Basil's cake. The cake is blessed and cut by the head of the household. One piece of cake is set aside in Basil's memory, and then the other pieces are passed to those gathered at the table. In one piece, a silver or gold coin is hidden. As the cake is eaten, there is great excitement to find out who will discover the coin and receive extra luck for the forthcoming year.

Children in Wales were also bearers of good wishes on New Year's Day. They roamed the village streets, carrying a jug of water and an evergreen sprig. They sprinkled all whom they met, wishing them the compliments of the season.

In the seventh century, January 1 became an official church holiday, with a mass being celebrated at the oldest Roman church, dedicated to the Mother of God. From that day forward, January 1 was also known as a holy day honoring Mary. Mary was given a new name: *Theotokos,* Greek for "God-bearer." In the tradition of her people, Mary and her husband, Joseph, bore Jesus to the temple on the eighth day after his birth to be signed with the mark of circumcision and to receive his name.

The fourth celebration connected with New Year's Day dates back to the sixth century: the Feast of the Holy Name of Jesus. The child of Mary and Joseph, born in the city of David, was given a holy name, a name that carried the promise of salvation. The prophets foretold the birth of this child. They called him, "Immanuel, God with us." They praised him as a wonderful Counselor, mighty God, everlasting Parent, Prince of Peace. His name was further heralded by an angel who spoke to Joseph in a dream. The child was to be called Jesus, "He who saves."

Each of these names bears an element of the New Year's Day story: a story that calls to mind a handmaiden bearing God's Child, who gave each of us a new beginning and named each a blessed child of God.

ENTERING THE STORY: IDEAS FOR FAMILY CELEBRATION

On this day of new beginnings, we have examined the names and traditions associated with the first day of the new year. It is a time to understand the privilege and importance of names and to celebrate the unique gift each person brings into the world God created.

1. Make Saint Basil's cake. Before putting the cake in the oven, hide a coin in the batter. Enjoy the discovery of who finds the coin and receives a special New Year's blessing.

2. Get a name book and find the meanings of the name of each family member. Discuss together whether the personality of each family member fits his or her name.

3. Have parents or others involved in naming tell the story of naming each child. What were the other names considered? How was the current name chosen?

4. If you have a genealogy chart or family Bible in your house, take it out and trace your lineage. Then read the names of Jesus' ancestors in the Gospels of Matthew and Luke.

5. Instead of making a normal New Year's resolution, choose a positive quality in the meaning of your name and decide how you will grow into that quality throughout the next year.

9

LEGENDS OF CHRISTMAS

January 2

God's words to Abraham, "Leave your country and go to a land that I am going to show you," begin our pilgrimage over the next three days of Christmas. They are not unlike Jesus' journey on this earth, leaving a heavenly realm and walking on foreign territory. The stories and cultures of the Old Testament provide a backdrop for understanding God's use of the culture and land into which Jesus was born to proclaim a message of peace and goodwill to all peoples, indeed to all of creation.

In the two-thousand-year history of humankind since Christ was born, numerous stories and legends have proclaimed the gift of the incarnation. Each speaks to a particular people at a particular time, sharing with them in their own languages and customs the good news of Jesus' birth.

As people of God, we need not fear how various cultures have adapted the story of Christmas or how the Christian story has adopted aspects of culture to proclaim this miracle. We are called to celebrate the power of God in delivering this message through and with these traditions.

SCRIPTURE

Genesis 12:1–3, 5–7

God said to Abram, "Go from your country and your kindred and your father's house to the land that I will show you. I will make of you a great nation, and I will bless you, and make your name great, so that you will be a blessing. I will bless those who bless you, and the one who curses you, I will curse; and in you all the families of the earth shall be blessed." When they had come to the land of Canaan, Abram passed through the land to the place at Shechem, to the oak of Moreh. At that time the Canaanites were in the land. Then God appeared to Abram and said, "To your offspring I will give this land." So he built there an altar to God, who had appeared to him.

YAMSHET'S GOLD

They removed the old man's body from the small house on the north side of Myra on the morning after his death. His eldest daughter, Chloe, stood at the doorway and watched as the wagon carried his casket to the cathedral for his funeral. It was not real for her yet. Late yesterday afternoon he had died. She came to his house immediately and prepared to receive the usual visitors, who would come as soon as they heard. Word traveled as quickly in this large town as if it were a small village. The house was full by early evening, and she had not grieved alone. One of her sisters was able to be there while the other sister, Phoebe, was living across the water on the island of Patmos. Phoebe would not get the news for weeks.

As the wagon rounded the corner, Chloe turned back into the house to close things up before she joined her family at the funeral Mass. The new bishop would be presiding. Although her father had always been close to the former bishop, Nicholas, who had died last year, her father was a man of little means, so she had been surprised last evening when the new bishop appeared at the house. He announced that Bishop Nicholas had left written instructions for this funeral. Her father was to receive the bishop's highest attention. She didn't completely understand, but she was pleased. So it would be.

After she straightened up the living area, she took one last trip into the little room where he had spent the last weeks of his life. She was flooded with the memory of the many acts of love she had received from this man throughout her life. She looked around at the gray walls of his last view of this world and grieved for their lack of beauty. As she looked at his cot, she saw a papyrus fragment laying where they had removed his body. It was wrinkled and compressed, as if he had been lying on it for many days. She picked it up and recognized his writing.

To the Bishop of Myra
The First Day of December in the Three Hundred and Forty-Second Year of Our Lord

Your Holiness,
I have waited all of my life to tell this story. Now I know that the time for telling has come. My days are few on this earth, so I must tell now or the story will never be told.

I have not told the story before because of a promise I made. . . . But let me start at the beginning.

My father was a wool merchant. My first taste of life was rich and privileged. As I grew, I learned the secrets of the wool trade. I traveled, bought wool, made proper business contacts, and was ready to take over the business when father died. My life was then blessed with a beautiful wife. Before long we were given three beautiful daughters. Life was exciting. Life was good. Life was solid.

When the girls were in their early teens, the fighting began in the east. At first I thought that I could find new routes to travel, but it became apparent that all routes were too dangerous. Over the period of one year, I lost my business, my house, and—in an unbelievable stroke of bad luck—my wife. Two days of fever and she was gone. At first I survived, feeding my three daughters and myself by selling the last of the wool scraps I had in my possession. Then one day, the scraps were gone. There was nowhere to turn and nothing to eat.

On the very day that I was about to give up, I was contacted by Yamshet, a rumored slave trader. He offered me a small bag of gold for the possession of

Chloe, my eldest daughter. It was unthinkable. I told him so and sent him away. A day later, when I was a day hungrier, he returned with a slightly smaller bag of gold. He assured me that she would be sold into a life better than starvation. He pointed through the window to Phoebe, my youngest, and observed how thin she was. He seemed glad to point out that she would not last long at that weight. "The fever will get her soon," he added. It must have been the talk of fever that started to convince me. I had known the power of fever. I asked him for one gold piece and three days to deliberate. He gladly complied.

On the morning of the third day, I awoke to gloom. The sun was shining, but my heart was filled with shadows. This was the day on which I was to sell my eldest daughter in order to save the lives of my other daughters. I had no choice. And yet I couldn't face the deed. When I entered our living area, there at the base of the window was a miracle. A large bag of gold. Twice as large as what Yamshet had offered. We were spared. I knelt and gave thanks to God, not knowing who else to thank.

The gold held us over for a few years. The fighting ended in the east, but I had no resources with which to get back in business. Shortly after Chloe was married and starting her own family, the gold ran out. The old hunger came back quickly. And so did Yamshet. There he was again with a bag of gold, offered this time for Ciel, my second daughter. I agonized. I knew that I had no option. I knew also that I could not expect another miracle. I asked again for three days deliberation. On the third morning, it was there, under the window: gold, enough to keep us alive for a long time.

Life became tough for the whole community over the next few years. Many people were hungry. We were blessed by the miracle. Ciel was married on the day the gold ran out. Yamshet was there within a week. Phoebe was the perfect age and a beautiful young woman, he told me. She would have a wonderful life if I would only sell her. If not, she would surely starve. It was not for the gold that I considered it. I would be left alone with that bag of gold, and it would be no good to me. I would gladly die to keep her from this fate. Yet her only options seemed to be slavery or starvation. I was a failure. I loathed myself for considering the sale, and I loathed myself for not being able to feed her. "Three days," Yamshet said as he flipped me a gold coin to live on. It felt heavy as I caught it.

On the third morning, I awoke before dawn. This time the gloom was not only within but also outside. As I stepped out of my sleeping room, I saw him: Nicholas, the one of Christ, the bishop's nephew. He was setting a large bag of gold in my window. He begged me to keep the secret. He had heard of my plight and was moved to help the family. He made me promise to keep the secret as long as he lived. I have done that.

As surely as God led the Israelites out of Egypt, Nicholas led me from total disintegration. It was not starvation that I feared, but it was the inability to convert my love for my daughters into action. Nicholas gave me that love to share. Those were not just bags of gold, but, as Nicholas put it, "God's love to share."

Bishop Nicholas lived long, doing many things for many people. I lie here now at the end of my life, a sinner who was inadequate for my family yet happy and whole because of these acts of Nicholas. Or, as he would say, acts of God.

My dear Bishop, may you carry on the work of this great man of God.

Faithfully,
Gorbyl of Myra

Chloe sat for a moment on the cot where her father died. Such love she had known from this man, her father. She now knew where it came from.

She took the fragment and walked toward the cathedral.

THE TRADITION

Saint Nicholas, Kriss Kringle, Sinter Klass, Santa Claus: four names for one person, one legend that most children in the world identify with Christmas. How did this fourth-century Bishop of Myra become the beloved carrier of the spirit of Christmas?

Historically, Saint Nicholas was born in Patara, a coastal town located in present-day Turkey. Even at a young age, he was devout. Under the tutelage of his uncle, he became quite interested in the church and entered the ministry. Nicholas was known for his kindness and generosity. The story for this day of the twelve is based on an incident early in Nicholas's life. He rescued the future fate of three daughters by secretly giving the destitute father three bags of gold.

As with many saints, stories of his good deeds and miracles spread throughout the countryside. His fame spread to Russia, Europe, and Lapland. Saint Nicholas was named the patron saint of Russia as protector of the weak and poor; the patron saint of boys, young men, and sailors in Greece and Sicily; and the patron saint of children in the Netherlands.

When Dutch immigrants traveled to America in the eighteenth century, they brought with them stories and Christmas customs of "Sinter Klass," which New York Dutch settlers called Saint Nicholas. Kriss Kringle was the name German immigrants called this man, "the Christ carrier." The tradition of gift-giving and caring for weak and poor children became the soil in which the legend of Santa Claus took root. Visual images of this kind soul took the shape of the Jultomten, a Swedish barn sprite that arrived on sleighs drawn by mountain goats at the winter solstice. One poet, Clement Moore, further shaped our current legend with the publication of " 'Twas the Night before Christmas" in 1823. The folk tradition of Santa Claus grew with the talents of two artists, Thomas Nast (late 1800s) and Haddon Sundblom (early 1920s Coca-Cola ads). The folk traditions of European cultures combined with the stories of a fourth-century Turkish saint to create a legend of both secular and sacred appeal.

A number of other traditional Christmas symbols drew their origins from pagan cultures.

Decorating an evergreen with lights is noted as early as the Middle Ages, and some accounts draw us back to the first century before Christ, during the festival of Saturnalia. The evergreens were a sign of everlasting life; the lights, a sign of the return of light to the earth after the winter solstice (the shortest day of the year). Because Christ was the light of the world and a source of everlasting life, these customs were carried on and interpreted by Christians. Martin Luther brought the tradition of a lighted tree into his German home after a walk in a star-studded sky. He saw the starlight reflected on the frosted trees outside his home. He was so inspired by the glory of God's heavens that he placed lighted candles on a tree to share that glory with his family.

Another Christmas evergreen, the holly, carries with it both a secular and sacred story. The English brought holly and ivy into their homes as signs of everlasting life and hope for the coming of spring. As Christianity grew, a legend also grew that told the story of how the crown of thorns that Jesus wore came from holly branches. As soldiers pressed the crown down, the white berries of the holly plant turned brilliant red with the shedding of Christ's blood.

An early Christian pope, Gregory the Great, wrote about sharing the good news of Christ with people from many cultures. He told his missionaries not to put down their customs "upon the sudden" but to adopt them "to the praise of God." Since the beginning of time, God has done the same, spoken to God's people over all the earth, in many languages, in many ways of praying, in many places. Christmas legends are all for the glory of God.

ENTERING THE STORY: IDEAS FOR FAMILY CELEBRATION

Individuals, families, communities, and cultures around the world draw deeply into their traditions to celebrate the Christmas holiday. Tree decorations, meals, and religious and secular pageants represent a few of the myriad ways in which the story of divine love has been made manifest.

1. Have each member of the family share his or her favorite Christmas tradition. If none of you knows the origin of these legends, go to the library to research them. Or better yet, take turns making up stories about their origin.

2. Celebrate the fullness of the Christmas tradition by gathering around the Christmas tree, singing carols. Start with "O Christmas Tree" and continue with other favorites.

3. Discover the culture of your own Christmas traditions. Find out if any traditional foods, rituals, or activities came from your ancestors' homeland (for example, eating *krummekake* or *fattigman* in Scandinavian families; sharing a greeting of peace and goodwill with the *opatik*, the Polish peace wafer).

4. Gather any Santa Claus ornaments and decorations and place them on your dining room table. See how much they reflect the origin of the Saint Nicholas tradition. Take advantage of after-Christmas sales. Search for something that reflects the original spirit of this Christmas legend.

5. Look for Christmas legends in other stories in this book. *(Hint: There are three others.)* Pick one for a bedtime story.

10

SACRED GROUND

January 3

Bethlehem was an ordinary place, a small village in Israel. The surrounding hills were home to sheep and shepherds. And a tiny cave held a stable that changed the nature of this village for centuries to come. Bethlehem became a place that held the extraordinary. It became a site of pilgrimage for thousands each year. And the tiny cave was covered with the edifice of a holy building; lanterns and eternal vigil lights burned over the place were Jesus was born.

Bethlehem stands among thousands of other sacred sights in Israel and around the world: places that are holy by their very nature, places that became holy because sacred events transpired there, and places that have been set aside to be holy. On this tenth day of Christmas, we look at places where God has been revealed.

SCRIPTURE

Genesis 28:11–13, 16–19

He came to a certain place and stayed there for the night, because the sun had set. Taking one of the stones of the place, he put it under his head and lay down in that place. And he dreamed that there was a ladder set up on the earth, the top of it reaching to heaven; and the angels of God were ascending and descending on it. And God stood beside him and said, "I am . . . the God of Abraham your father and the God of

Isaac; the land on which you lie I will give to you and to your offspring." Then Jacob woke from his sleep and said, "Surely God is in this place— and I did not know it." And he was afraid, and said, "How awesome is this place. This is none other than the house of God, and this is the gate of heaven." So Jacob rose early in the morning, and he took the stone that he had put under his head and set it up for a pillar and poured oil on the top of it. He called that place Bethel.

AN ORDINARY PLACE

The large door swung shut behind Stephen and immediately cut off the noise of the downtown street. He was amazed at the silence he heard as he stood in the entryway, dwarfed by the door he had just passed through and dwarfed by the door in front of him. It was Friday afternoon, and he had put off this stop for the entire week. Now, with all of his other work orders completed, it was time to do this job.

Stephen was in his last year in college and had found a summer job with a small cabinetmaking firm. He had helped his father in the same type of work throughout his youth, so his skills were apparent on the first day of the summer job. Stephen's father had always called him the "finish-work man," and he now carried this skill into this summer job. Within one week on the job, the boss had seen his finishing skills and had assigned him to follow the other crews around to sand, stain, and varnish. He liked the work. He could see the final transformation of every project from "rough" to "complete." It was Stephen who was the last to leave a job. It was Stephen who heard the final acclamations of approval. It was Stephen who usually worked alone while the other crew members went on to another project.

It was Stephen who now stood alone in the narthex of Saint Louis Catholic Church in the heart of a busy city. He had never been comfortable in churches. His family hadn't gone to church very much in his youth. Weddings and funerals were his only experience with churches, and he had always felt uncomfortable at those events. There were too many things he didn't understand, too many strange names for things, and too much standing and kneeling. So Stephen stayed away. He had stayed away from this job all week, but now the time had come.

Stephen took the work order from the folder he carried. "Report to the rectory for instructions," it said on the bottom. He wasn't sure what a rectory was. He decided to go back outside and ask at the little house that was attached to the church. As he stepped back out onto the busy downtown street, he felt relief at not having to go through the big doors that led him into the main part of the church. That struck him as strange because he had been growing weary of spending most of his time in the noise and busyness of the downtown district. Now, when he had just been surrounded with incredible quiet, he was relieved to get back out into a normal world. He smelled the diesel exhaust of a bus pulling noisily away from the bus stop as he knocked on the door of the little church house.

He was glad he hadn't asked about the rectory. When the door opened, a short man, dressed in dark clothes, answered. When the man spotted the Roan's Cabinetmaking insignia on Stephen's shirt, he smiled brightly. The brightness of the smile was balanced by the white collar, which Stephen hadn't seen until that moment.

"You must be here to finish the new altar rail. I'm Father Bourassa," the man said. "I've been worried that you wouldn't get here before the weekend. I'd hoped to have the project done before the weekend masses. The rail is, of course, in the church. I'm in a meeting just now, but you can pull your truck up to the back door in the alley and find your way in. I'll unlock the door, and you can let yourself in. Lock it again behind you. I'll check on you later."

With that, the door was closed, and Stephen stood alone again on the street. "The church," Stephen thought. "How am I going to work all day in there? It'll be damp, gloomy, and quiet and I'll probably have a bunch of statues watching me."

When he got into his truck to pull around back, he was struck with the heat. In just a few minutes, the truck had become unbearably hot. It took Stephen fifteen minutes of fighting the downtown traffic just to pull around into the alley. Cross-traffic had been so busy that even when the corner light changed, grid-lock prevented him from proceeding. Red, green, red, green. "I can't go yet," Stephen grumbled. After another red and another green, he finally was able to turn the corner, only to find the alley blocked by a delivery truck. He sat, waiting and getting warmer while the delivery man crawled back into his truck and took out a clipboard. "Can't the guy do that when he gets out on the street?" Stephen thought. "He'll have plenty of time sitting in traffic with things as busy as they are today."

Finally he was clear and found his way to the back door of the church. He parked the truck, grabbed some supplies, and made his way through a long hallway to the main part of the church. Stephen stopped at the entrance, took a breath, and stepped inside. It wasn't damp, but it was cool. It felt good. He walked up to the rail that he was supposed to refinish. Each step he took echoed off the ceiling high above. He had the sense that he was not alone. He wasn't. There were several people scattered around the pews, just sitting or kneeling and praying. He wondered if he could work with them being there. "Got to get the job done," he shrugged and went up to check the machine sanding. Most of the sanding had been done by the crew ahead of him, but there was always a little hand sanding left for him. He rubbed his hand on the fresh oak rail, looking for rough spots. The oak felt good. It felt strange to be in so large a place and still be in such quiet. He found an area that needed sanding and went to work. The sound of the sandpaper smoothing wood rang out with each stroke. At first it seemed like a rude sound in all that silence, and then Stephen began to feel soothed by the familiar sanding rhythm. "Maybe this is my prayer," Stephen joked with himself. "I can't kneel and mutter to God but I will sand this rail."

When the sanding was done, he put on the first coat of varnish. Tomorrow morning he would come and sand out any rough spots, put on another coat, and be done for the weekend. The priest would have his rail ready for Sunday. Stephen made his way out the back hall and left the church behind. The world was still there, hot and busy.

Saturday morning traffic was not bad as Stephen returned to the church, so he parked his truck on the street and carried his supplies in both hands through the large front doors. He walked through the narthex and pushed the large doors open to the church with his back. He stopped and turned to listen for the quiet. It was there. The church was still cool. It felt good. It was nice to be off the street again. There was no one praying this morning, so he could work alone. As Stephen walked up the long aisle, he heard the echo of his footsteps. He didn't feel alone. He stopped and looked around. There was no one else in the church. He didn't quite know what to make of this feeling. This morning, the church was more than just a workplace: It felt like a sanctuary, a place of peace here in the middle of the busy city. He wasn't sure what the presence that he sensed was. He couldn't say that it wasn't God. He knew that he wasn't going to kneel down and pray or anything, but he liked this place, and he liked this feeling. He paused near the front of the church and rested. He rested from the noise. He rested from the traffic. He rested from his busy life.

Then it was time to begin again. He walked to the altar rail and ran his hand along yesterday's varnish. Near the middle, he found a rough spot. He began to sand again.

THE TRADITION

Bethlehem, Mount Horeb, Rome, Jerusalem, Lourdes, Guadalupe: places of pilgrimage for Christians around the world, holy places where the Word of God was revealed, places where the Creator met creation. These sacred places are among thousands of sites where people of faith gather for rituals of renewal and healing, contemplation, and rites of passage. They are places to sing and dance, to pray and retell the stories of where God met humankind in word and deed, places to dwell within the quiet peace of the spirit.

The Christmas season is replete with stories of pilgrimages to holy places. From the story of Mary and Joseph returning to the city of David, to the presentation of Jesus in the Temple at Jerusalem, scripture readings during the twelve days of Christmas make known the places where God was revealed—sacred ground.

On December 29 and 30, the gospel readings tell the story of Mary and Joseph taking Jesus to the Temple to be circumcised and dedicated to God (Luke 2:22–40). On December 31, we hear the story of the holy family journeying to Jerusalem for the Passover Feast at the Temple (Luke 2:42–52). For the Jewish people, the Temple was sacred ground. It had been set aside to be holy, to be a place where the faithful gathered, offered sacrifices, and made petitions. Our own churches are holy ground. They are intentionally set aside to offer the faithful, the seeker, and the weary a place of rest and refreshment. As families gather on Christmas Eve and Christmas Day to celebrate the birth of the incarnate God, they are making a pilgrimage to holy ground. And the music, the Word, and the sacrament are means of affirming that relationship with God, the God who was revealed to the world two thousand years ago.

Today's text tells of a place that became holy because a sacred event transpired there. When Jacob came upon "a certain place" (Gen. 28:10–22), he laid down to rest and dreamed. His vision of a ladder extending from heaven to earth caused him to know God had visited him at this place. Upon waking, Jacob dedicated the place to God by setting up a stone pillar as a symbol of God's presence, a memorial to that sacred event. Jacob then anointed it with oil, consecrating the ground and renaming it Bethel, which means "the house of God."

In the Middle and Far East, the mountains and valleys are covered with shrines dedicated to places where humankind has come into contact with the divine. The Holy Land itself is a monument to the walk of Jesus on this earth. Thousands walk the *Via Dolorosa,* the Way of the Cross, and visit the churches that have been dedicated to the events of Christ's life: the

Church of the Nativity, the Church of the Beatitudes, the Church of the Ascension.

Other stories told during the twelve days of Christmas reveal places where the ground, by its very nature, is sacred. On January 2, the story of Abraham entering the promised land is told (Gen. 12:1–7). He comes upon a Canaanite sanctuary, the oak of Moreh at Shechem. God revealed his promises to Abraham at this sight. And sensing the holiness of the place, Abraham, as his Canaanite predecessors had done, built an altar to God on this very site. On January 4, the Old Testament reading tells the story of Moses and the burning bush on Mount Horeb (Exod. 3:1–15). Mount Horeb was probably a Midianite sacred place. On this holy mountain, God spoke to Moses: "Take off your shoes. You are standing on holy ground." The removal of sandals before entering a holy place was an ancient custom.

Much of our understanding of the world of God comes from an acceptance of the world of spirit. These Christmas texts speak to that world, making its presence known in the physical world which God created. Upon holy ground, God's presence is made known in ways that we—as physical beings—can feel, touch, and remember. God made the earth sacred upon its creation. God entered that world in the incarnation. God continually reveals the divine presence to that world through sacred time and sacred space. This is holy ground.

ENTERING THE RITUAL: IDEAS FOR FAMILY CELEBRATION

The celebration of Christmas is rooted in the concept of sacred place. We remember the story of how a tiny village named Bethlehem became a place of pilgrimage. We visit sacred places as we enter churches to honor the birth of the Christchild. The following activities share other ways to experience sacred space.

1. On this day, take a family pilgrimage. Travel to a number of churches in your city or town. Enter these places, aware of the fact that they have been set aside to be holy.

2. Find someone in your congregation or community who has traveled to the Holy Land. Invite her or him to dinner and hear stories of a journey to a sacred place.

3. Decide if there is a sacred space in your house. If so, where is it, and why is it sacred? If not, how can you create one? For some, it is the kitchen table, where the family always gathers. For others, it may be a quiet, candlelit corner.

4. Many people in a community know of natural places with a sacred quality (waterfalls, canyons, pine groves, beaches, mountaintops). Ask around, then plan a family expedition to one of those areas today.

5. After you come home from church, discuss how you act differently in sacred space (for example, how you move, how you speak, how you listen).

11

And Heaven and Nature Sing

January 4

Christmas choirs and congregations sing a new song to God as they gather each December to celebrate the birth of Jesus. On Christmas Day, we hear the story of God entering the very world God created. With the incarnation, God affirmed creation. On this day of the Christmas season, we hear the world's response: creation affirming God. "While fields and floods, rocks, hills, and plains repeat the sounding joy."[1]

Through psalms and songs, humankind gives witness to the music and majesty with which the earth responds to God in a lofty, gleaming mountain peak standing against the blue sky. And the song of a river bubbling and roaring in celebration of the spring melt. And what if not praise is the beauty of an individual snowflake, joined in chorus by thousands of other snowflakes, similar but each unique in its witness to God's diversity?

On this eleventh day of the Christmas season, we discover the response of the earth, giving praise to the glory of God in songs and carols.

SCRIPTURE

Psalm 98:1, 4–9

O sing to God a new song, for God has done marvelous things! Make a joyful noise to God, all the earth; break forth into joyous song and sing praises. Sing praises to God with the lyre, with the lyre and the sound of melody. With trumpets and the sound of the horn make a joyful noise before the Ruler, the Sovereign. Let the sea roar, and all that fills it; the world and those who live in it. Let the floods clap their hands; let the hills sing together for joy at the presence of God; for God is coming to judge the earth. God will judge the world with righteousness, and the peoples with equity.[2]

SONG OF THE EARTH

"Long in bed," Isaac thought as he swung his feet to the floor. "Once a luxury and now a daily routine," he pondered as he began the slow chore of getting himself ready for his daily world. That world had been severely limited for the last seven years. He had once been the pastor of the Independent Church in Mark Lane, a large church in London. His illness now limited his days and nights to his rooms in the residence of Sir Thomas Abbey. His activities were limited to reading and writing. Staying in bed late in the morning, dressing, eating, and studying God's word. "Not a bad life," he sometimes conceded. His only real limitation, he would console himself, was the limitation of his mind and spirit.

As he stood to dress, thunder crashed outside, so powerful that it shook the window pane. Isaac walked over to the window and looked out at a dim morning. This murkiness was different from the natural, comforting darkness of the evening. It didn't belong in the middle of the morning. Coaches were clattering in the streets. The markets were full. School children were at their lessons. In the middle of an ordinary day, the world of nature was now changing the rules.

Isaac saw the woman across the yard lighting a lamp. He turned back to begin his work for the morning. He was writing on the psalms. Shadows had crept in. He found that he couldn't work without a lamp. He returned to the window. As he looked out again, the sky was green and purple at the same time. Up the street, people scurried for cover. He opened the window. The air was still and moist. The smell of a new garden was carried in the still air. He waited for the downpour.

Isaac remembered another storm. Long ago his father and he had to pull their coach off the road to wait out a thunderstorm. They pulled up to the undercut bank of a stream. His father covered the horses' heads to prevent their startling at the lightning. They both sat on a rock, protected by the tall bank. The rain fell hard, pelting the surface of the river. Soon a curtain of water fell from the bank over their heads, just missing their feet as it made its way to the river. As the storm passed, the sun broke through the clouds and light flashed on the water that was still falling at their feet.

"Look, Father, rainbows," Isaac said joyfully.

"Look and listen, Isaac," his father responded. "The earth is responding to God's gift of rain."

Isaac listened. The stream, silent when they stopped, now chortled, full of new rain. The birds sang with newfound happiness in the fresh, wet world after the rain. A breeze whispered through the treetops, and raindrops captured on their leaves fell with a sigh as they completed their path to the ground.

"It is praise, Isaac," his father said. "The earth can teach us the purest form of God's praise. It naturally responds to God's gifts. This is the sound of purest praise."

Isaac stood now, many years later and waited for the rain. A drop hit the window, then another. Then it began. The lightning was now past. The rain fell in waves, shaking the leaves in the trees, filling the low spots in the paths and washing everything in Isaac's sight. The murkiness was now past. He felt joy at this renewed show of God's majesty. He sat at his study table and read:

> *Roar, sea, and every creature in you:*
> *Sing, earth, and all who live on you!*
> *Clap your hands, you rivers;*
> *you hills, sing together with joy before God.*
>
> —Psalm 98

THE TRADITION

The Christmas favorite "Joy to the World" was an inspiration. In reading Psalm 98, Isaac Watts fashioned this much-loved Christmas hymn in 1719, as a piece in his hymn collection *Psalms of*

David. The opening measures of the "Gloria" in Handel's *Messiah* influenced Lowell Mason in creating the tune for this carol. With "Joy to the World," Watts and Mason gave voice to the strains of praise that rise from the earth itself in celebration of the cosmic scope of salvation announced in John 3:16: "For God so loved the world."

Isaac Watts (1674–1748) was an English theologian and hymnmaker born in Southampton, England. In his early adult years, he composed a number of hymns and is credited with being the originator of the modern hymn, distinct from the chants and medieval melodies of his day. Watts composed over six hundred hymns, including "Our God, Our Help in Ages Past" and "When I Survey the Wondrous Cross." As a minister, he was a renowned and passionate preacher, absorbed in the mysteries of God. Psalm 98 is a fitting expression of his theology. It is one of the enthronement psalms in the Old Testament, most likely part of a temple liturgy which heralded the New Year. Its verses call upon all of creation to praise God.

Over the centuries, other musicians have created songs that have upheld this very theme. Marcus Prudentius (348–413) was an early Christian poet. His most extensive work was a collection of twelve poems, one for each hour of the day. His ninth poem, "*Corde Natus*," is the Christmas hymn "Of the Father's Love Begotten." This hymn captures the message of John's prologue in the Fourth Gospel. Its reads, "Of the Father's love begotten, Ere the worlds began to be; He is Alpha and Omega, He the source, the ending he."

Images of the earth are used to convey the promise of the Messiah in the traditional German carol, "Lo! How a Rose E'er Blooming." The text for this hymn was taken from a sixteenth-century prayer book from St. Alban's Carthusian monastery. Local folklore language "amid the cold of winter" combines with the prophet Isaiah's imagery of the "rose" and the "stem of Jesse" to pronounce the birth of the world's Savior. Modern songwriter Royce J. Scherf composed "The Hills Are Bare at Bethlehem" in 1973 as a gift to his congregation. It, too, uses images of the earth to convey the message of salvation: "From earth's old dust a greenwood stem."

The heavens also tell the glory of God. "Angels from the Realm of Glory" was written by James Montgomery (1771–1854), an English hymnmaker. The fourth verse was added as a Doxology, praising the God of all creation: "All creation join in praising, God the Father, Spirit, Son; Evermore your voices raising, to the eternal Three in One."

A number of Christmas hymns speak to the role of the Bethlehem star in guiding the Magi to the stable. "The First Noel," a seventeenth-century English carol, replaced the psalm at the Christmas Day service in Protestant West England. "Bright and Glorious Is the Sky" was written for Christmas Day in 1810 by the great Danish hymnmaker Nikolai Grundtvig.

Through the works of these poets and musicians, we hear the message of Christmas Day proclaimed in a new way: Joy to the world. Joy from the world. Amen.

ENTERING THE RITUAL: IDEAS FOR FAMILY CELEBRATION

Scripture abounds with verses that speak of the response of creation to the Creator. It is recorded in psalms and parables, in images from Genesis to Revelation. The beauty and diversity of the earth mirrors the beauty and the diversity of the Creator. Many of these images are recorded in the sounds of the earth, and the sounds of the earth have been interpreted by various composers.

1. Hike to a natural area and listen to the music of creation. If you live near the ocean, hear it roar. If you live near a river, hear it clap. If you live among hills or mountain valleys, hear them sing. Read aloud Psalm 98 in this symphony of nature's response.

2. Gather around a piano at your house, or your neighbor's, and sing the songs of creation heralding the Christmas event: "Joy to the World," "Friendly Beasts," "Lo! How a Rose E'er Blooming," and "Angels from the Realm of Glory."

3. In the quiet of your living room, listen to Beethoven's *Pastoral Symphony*, Dvorak's *New World Symphony*, or Copeland's

Appalachian Spring. Focus on the praise of nature which these composers have discovered.

4. Behold the beauty and diversity of nature as a testimony of praise to the Creator. Take a piece of black construction paper and put it in your freezer for a few minutes; then take it outside to catch new-fallen snow. As the snowflakes collect on your paper, witness the uniqueness of each individual flake. If you live in an area without snow, take a hike to a wooded area. Find the places on the trees where the leaves of last year fell off. Look at all the different markings (leaf scars) of various scrubs and trees. Use your imagination to see the faces of people or animals in these images.

5. Before you go to bed, take your family or friends outside and gaze upon the universe. "When I look at your heavens, the work of your fingers, the moon and the stars, what are human beings that you are mindful of them, mortals that you care for them?" (Ps. 8:3–4)

6. Retell the story of the star of Bethlehem (Matt. 2) and remember how something God created pointed the way to three travelers in search of the Savior of the universe.

12

THE BLESSING OF THE WATERS

January 5

Water: It holds life in a mother's womb; it draws forth life, as spring fields green with rebirth: it cleanses both body and soul in a person's journey through this world.

As the Christmas season nears its end, we turn away from the manger at Bethlehem, where a few of the faithful beheld the Savior. We turn toward the world as the very waters of creation are used in proclaiming the walk of the Creator on the earth: "This is my beloved Son." With Jesus' baptism in the River Jordan, the waters of the earth were sanctified as Jesus, the Word made flesh, immersed himself and rose to draw forth new life in each of the creatures he encountered.

SCRIPTURE

Matthew 3:13, 16–17

Jesus came from Galilee to John at the Jordan, to be baptized by him.... And when Jesus had been baptized, just as he came up from the water, suddenly the heavens were opened to him and he saw the Spirit of God descending like a dove and alighting on him. And a voice from heaven said, "This is my Child, the Beloved, with whom I am well pleased."

EPIPHANY SOUP

In three days Jennifer would return home from the city. At first when she came to spend her last week of Christmas vacation with her aunt Valerie, she had been afraid of the city. Now she was beginning to like it. Each day she saw new things and did new things. Subways, taxis, and doormen now felt exciting to her rather than just intimidating. She and Val had seen department stores and museums. Today Val took her along to work. She spent half of the day looking out from Val's thirty-sixth floor window. Jennifer pretended that she was on her own and in her own office. This week had been fun. She wasn't really ready for the visit to end.

"Let's head back to the apartment, Jenny," Val declared as she gathered some papers and stuffed them in her briefcase. "We've got some work to do to get ready for church tonight."

"Church on Friday night?" Jenny responded with curiosity and some dismay. "We never have church on Fridays."

Val smiled and said, "Tomorrow is Epiphany. We have a special service on the eve of Epiphany." She grabbed her coat and continued, "Tonight we will go to the Blessing of the Waters. It's one of my favorite times of the year."

After they finished the evening dishes, Val went to the dining room buffet and brought out two tall pottery containers that had rubber seals on top. She took them to the sink and filled them with water. "We'll take these for the blessing."

Jenny sat silently, confused about the evening events.

As they got out of the taxi, Jenny looked up the church steps that came right down to the sidewalk. Her eyes passed the doors and took in the entire front of the church building. It was not the biggest church that she had seen on her visit. At the top, where the steeple should be, there was a large green dome which stretched up into a point. "It looks like an onion," Jenny whispered to Val.

"Lets go inside," Val said as they scaled the steps.

They entered the church with a group of people. "There are no pews," Jenny stated quietly.

"We stand while we are here. We even move around a little bit," Val whispered to Jenny. "Standing together is a part of our participation."

The church seemed dim to Jenny. Along the sides were pictures, stark and colorful, with candles burning beneath them. Val led her over to one, bought a candle and lit it, then stood in silence. Jenny stood, too. People were moving along the sides of the church. Candles flickered. People were silent. The pictures danced in the candlelight. Jenny looked around and felt like she was in a very special world.

As they moved away from the picture, Jenny dared to ask, "Who are those people in the pictures?"

"Saints and other believers," Val responded. "The pictures are called 'icons.' As we pray, these icons remind us of the whole company of heaven that is praying with us. Those people have gone before us, but they still worship God. The icons are a reminder of the constant meeting of heaven and earth."

"It feels a little like heaven in here," Jenny said quietly. Val smiled and faced the door for the entrance procession.

The next two hours were a swirl of sights, sounds, and smells which blended together for Jenny: the entrance of the worship leaders with their elaborate clothes, each carrying a tall, thin candle; the sweet swirl of incense, which made Jenny feel even more like she was in the clouds of heaven; the screen at the front with three doors through which the priest came and went; and the ongoing chanting, which sounded strange to Jenny at first and then began to pick up her spirit and carry it through the worship.

At some point near the middle of the service, the priest came and blessed all of the water that was stored in the great variety of vessels placed at the front. Jenny watched the two they had brought and paid special attention when he blessed them. There was so much to watch! The music continued. People moved around a little. Many of the people participated in the Eucharist, and then, almost suddenly, they were leaving. Jenny was amazed to discover that although she had been standing for the entire two hours, her feet were not really very tired.

Val picked up their water containers at the front of the church. As they were going down the church stairs to the sidewalk, she handed one to Jenny. It was the same container they had brought, yet Jenny was even more careful when she received it from Val. She caught a whiff of incense as they reached the sidewalk. "Maybe it's coming from these water jugs," she thought. The smell carried the memories of the last two hours back to Jenny. She felt as if she had been in another world, in a sacred place. Now, with this blessed water in her arms, she was carrying something of that world home with her.

Even the utilitarian interior of the taxi seemed different now that they carried this precious cargo. At home Jenny carried the jar carefully through the halls, up the elevator, and into the apartment. She followed the lead of her aunt and set it on the counter. She stepped back, looked at the two vessels of blessed water on the counter, and stood in awe. Then a question entered her mind.

"What do you do with this water, Aunt Val?" she said with a sudden curiosity. She had an image of the jars sitting on the dining room buffet or another spot of honor.

"Soup," Val said with a subtle smile. "First, I will use some of it to make Epiphany soup for us tomorrow. Then I'll use some of it to give the house a good cleaning. I always wash a few clothes with it . . ."

"You can use normal water for those things," Jenny exclaimed before Val could finish. "This is very special water, holy water. I don't think we should use it for everyday things like eating and cleaning."

Val laughed. "That's exactly the point, Jenny. Water is a part of everyday life. God blesses water. In doing so, God blesses our lives—not just our worship lives, but our eating, our cleaning, our getting dressed in the morning."

Jenny paused. She remembered the feeling she had when she caught the last scent of the incense at the base of the church steps. A sweet memory of being closer to God's world. She thought about the thrill she had while she stood in the elevator and had her arms wrapped around that jar of sacred water. "Won't God be upset if we use this special water for everyday things?"

Val stood and led Jenny into the guest room. They stood at Jenny's suitcase. "Get me that pink sweatshirt that you tend to wear too often," Val said. "I'll wash it with a few other things in the water that has been blessed. God won't be upset. God gave us this sacred water for a sacred purpose: so we can carry its blessing into our everyday lives."

Jenny handed her the shirt. She decided that she would wear this shirt, specially cleaned, for her first day back in school.

THE TRADITION

Two thousand years before Christ was born, the Egyptians celebrated the eve of the winter solstice, honoring the birth of their god Osiris from Kore the virgin. They believed the waters of the Nile held miraculous powers on that holy night, turning to wine as the night fell.

In the desert lands to the north and centuries later, the Israelites dreamed of another miraculous event with water. The prophet Isaiah proclaimed to those in exile that water would gush forth in the desert, streams in the wasteland, and that the scorched earth would become a lake. And along the banks of the River Jordan, six hundred years after Isaiah, the Child of God stepped forth, was baptized, and forever consecrated the waters of the earth by being immersed in them.

These three events took place in lands of little rain and little water. In the ancient Middle East, water was a prized possession. It was both bought and sold. As such, water was regarded as both a sign and symbol of God's saving power. In the modern world, water is seen as the lifeblood of the earth, the one source that brings life to the entire planet. For both the ancient and modern world, water is a blessing, a sustainer, and giver of life.

Churches in the Eastern tradition of Christianity observe January 5 and 6 as the Blessing of the Waters. The appointed reading for this day tells of the baptism of Jesus in the River Jordan. As Jesus' divinity was pronounced, there was a subsequent sanctification of the waters by the Savior's immersion in them. Saint John Chrysostom, in the year 387, delivered a homily with this understanding: "For this is the day on which He was baptized and sanctified the natures of the waters. Therefore also on this solemnity in the middle of the night, all who are gathered, having drawn the water, set the liquid aside in their houses and preserve it throughout the year, for today, the waters are sanctified."[1] An Orthodox liturgy for this day proclaimed, "Today through the presence of the Lord the waters of the Jordan River are changed into remedies; today the whole universe is refreshed with mystical streams."[2]

By the sixth century, in communities along the Mediterranean Sea and in many towns and villages where rivers and lakes formed a basis for their livelihood, Christians gathered to remember this day and this event. The faithful proceeded from the church in the late-night hours to nearby rivers and seashores, where the minister immersed the cross into the water three times, reminiscent of Jesus' immersion in the River Jordan and of the three times a child is immersed in the waters of baptism:

> May the blessings of the Jordan be upon this water! May the blessings of the Jordan be upon this water! May the blessings of the Jordan be upon this water! And may we who partake of it be cleansed and purified, blessed and sanctified, healed and made whole, so that we may be filled with fullness of God who is all in all.[3]

In some communities, they went out in boats and scattered aromatic substances into the water. They drew the water into jars and urns to use later in their homes and in their fields.

The prayers recited on this evening of celebration form litanies of praise for the gift of all of creation. Prayers are said for the light of the sun, the radiance of the moon, the clouds that shower justice, and the whole of the universe being refreshed with streams of flowing water.

The immersion of God in the waters of the Jordan are a lingering witness to the mystery of an omnipotent God becoming flesh and renewing the face of the earth.

ENTERING THE RITUAL: IDEAS FOR FAMILY CELEBRATION

In creating the world, God brought forth the ordinary through extraordinary means. God created soil, water, plants, and animals by the power of God's Word. In sending the Savior to earth, God used an ordinary event—the birth of a child—to bring about the miraculous renewal of creation, of all that was created in the beginning. On the eve of the last day of the Christmas season, we remember how God uses ordinary means to bring forth new life.

1. Find out when each member of your family was baptized. Take the new calendar for the new year and mark those baptismal anniversaries along with birthdays and anniversaries.

2. Remember the day when you were called to be a child of God. Take an ordinary bowl from your kitchen and fill it with water. Read the story of Jesus' baptism. Then have one member of your family (the oldest or youngest) break off a small sprig from the Christmas tree. Dipping the branch in the water, have them sprinkle each family member with water, saying, "In the name of the Father, Son, and the Holy Spirit." This sprinkling with an evergreen sprig is a sign of God's ever-living promise, brought to us in the waters of baptism.

3. Fill up a pot with tap water. As a family, choose other gifts from God's earth (beans, potatoes, onions, beef, or chicken). Make an Epiphany Eve soup as the main course for the evening meal. As you say a table grace, be thankful not only for the soup you eat but for all the waters of the world.

4. Examine the uses of water in your household. Look for ways to protect and preserve the gift of water in your lives by more careful use.

5. Each time you use the faucet (to bathe, cook, clean, or get a drink), say a simple prayer of thanksgiving.

EPIPHANY

January 6

Light: This is the central image of this day. It is a day set aside to remember the coming of light in the sign of the star to the Magi in the ancient Near East. They were drawn by dreams and the heavens to bear witness to the birth of a king. But this day is not a celebration of an earthly monarch. It is the world's recognition of the coming of the Child of God—the one with God in the creation of the universe.

We end our reflections on the twelve days of Christmas by returning to the light heralded in the Christmas gospel, the story about the light shining in obscurity and coming into the world. Today we celebrate the world receiving the light in the faces of the Magi. We listen to the story of humankind recognizing its need for God, and turning from the dimness of human knowledge and wisdom to journey toward the light of Christ.

SCRIPTURE

Isaiah 60:1–3

Arise, shine; for your light has come, and the glory of God has risen upon you. For shadows shall cover the earth, and thick shadows the peoples; but God will arise upon you, and God's glory will appear over you. Nations shall come to your light and rulers to the brightness of your dawn.

OUT OF THE NIGHT

Thursday was the day of first ice. It came late that year. The fall had been mild. The ice attempted to settle on the lake and was blown away several times before the ice cover finally stayed. On Sunday the cover settled and froze solid. By Thursday it was three inches thick—frozen thick enough to stand on, frozen early enough in the season to catch walleyes in the second channel of the Wisepi chain of lakes. Two of the guys at Harold's shop had been out from midafternoon until midnight on both Thursday and Friday nights, and had limited out every line in the water. They knew what to do when they came off the ice: Call Harold.

Harold was obsessed with firsts when it came to ice fishing. First on the ice, first fish, first limit, and first to get an ice house positioned for the winter. This year, they were happy to inform him, there was only one first left for him to achieve: the ice house. Three of his annual firsts were unattainable, so the idea of skidding his pink, three-person ice house out to its familiar spot on the channel stuck in his mind like an advertising jingle that he could not shake. He would have to get out on the lake tomorrow. He would use the kids to slide the house out.

Harold loaded the Chevy wagon with ice skates, hockey sticks, fishing equipment, and Peter and Ellen, his two youngest kids. Both were fast approaching their teenage years. His brother Hjalmer would remove the house from its summer place behind the garage, load it onto his pickup truck, and meet them at the lakes. Hjalmer's son David would be along to help skid the house.

The house skidded easily. There was little snow, and the ice had frozen with a smooth surface. The only irregularities were long waves which stood frozen, parallel to the eastern shore. They looked as if they had been stopped short in their journey toward the rocks. "Heaves" Hjalmer called them, waves thrust upward by the expansion of the ice; waves of cold, not wind; waves that would never reach the shore. They skidded the house all the way out between two of the heaves, pushing it up and over one of them just as they reached the channel. The holes were drilled easily; the ice was not thick yet. Harold and Hjalmer began rigging the lines while the three kids ran back to the car and laced on skates.

The skating began with hockey. Two minutes passed, and Ellen set down her stick and skated over to the nearest frozen wave. She sidestepped to the top of the crest and then glided gently down the other side. She circled out about ten yards and then skated back, slowly at first, but increasing speed as she approached the heave. As she reached the wave, she hunkered down, grabbed her ankles, slid up the small rise, and launched herself off of the top of the heave. She flew like a barrel jumper. She landed hard, but not so hard. She turned back for another pass.

Peter joined her. He began his approach to the swell by dropping his hockey stick and continuously increased speed until he hit the wave.

"Fourteen barrels you cleared," David shouted. "I'll bet I can clear fifteen."

The barrel jumping continued with an occasional argument about the number of imaginary barrels cleared. In the middle of an argument about whether it is even possible to jump twenty-two barrels, Ellen took the lead again and began to cruise along the top of the widest swell, slowly at first until she saw the boys following. She was headed toward the next channel and the entrance to the third lake. She was the last to get there. She was passed by Peter, then David, as the three of them became long-distance racers, focused on the undefined goal. The race was forgotten somewhere in the channel.

As they entered the third lake in the chain, a fallen tree blocked their passage. It was too high to jump, and drifted snow blocked the underside. Peter and David boosted themselves up with some effort, but Ellen was totally grounded.

"We're a team," Peter said simply as he and David each grabbed an arm to hoist her into a stomach slide over the trunk and into the snow.

The team pushed onward through at least two more channels before they found the county park called the "Homestead

Museum." It was closed in the winter, but they had all visited this park in the summer with their parents. It was different now: The quiet white of winter made the place seem new. They were the first to be here since late fall, but to them it seemed as if they were the first *ever* to be here. Like the first homesteaders, they stood on new land. They were homesteaders now, settling a new frontier. Peter found that one of the buildings was open. It was a shed—not the actual house, but close enough.

Inside was a different world: colder, dimmer, and of another time. It was so easy to leave their time. They went back to the first time anyone had stood in this cabin. It was theirs. And they, for a few moments, belonged to it and to another time: a time of excitement, a time of courage, of leaving roots and building a new land. The time of pioneers.

"It's getting dark fast," Peter said. "Dad is going kill us if we don't get back to the ice house before nightfall. We'll be in real trouble."

Ellen knew instantly when she stepped out of the shed that she was in another kind of trouble. In the fading light, she couldn't tell which direction to go.

"Do you know the way back, Peter?" she almost whispered.

Peter pulled his red knit cap over his ears and said, "That's easy. We just go back the way we came. Follow me."

They passed through a channel, along the shoreline of the next lake and into the next channel. As they entered the next lake, Ellen noticed it first. "This is the homestead cabin. We haven't gone anywhere."

Peter responded, "That must have been the last lake in the chain. We circled it and came back to this place. Now we know that we are going in the right direction. All we need to do is skate."

And skate is what they did. Numb fingers, sore ankles, and probably in trouble with their dads, they skated through the night. Past the fallen tree, through what felt like channel after channel they skated. They were no longer barrel jumpers, explorers, or homesteaders. They were just kids. Tired, cold, and a little worried about what their dads would say.

Finally as they passed through yet another channel they saw the light of what had to be the ice house. Peter skated fastest, so he got there first. The door swung open, and warm lantern light fell out onto the lonely ice.

As Peter and David stepped into the house, Ellen stopped just short of the spot where the light fell on the ice. She wasn't afraid of being in trouble. She certainly didn't want to stay out in the cold night any longer. She stopped for a moment to anticipate her step out of the shadowy cold into warmth and light.

THE TRADITION

Historically, the celebration of the Epiphany is older than Christmas. Christmas originated in the Western church during the fourth century. The festival of the Epiphany can be traced to the late second century in Egypt. On this day, the appearance of God was told through three stories: the visit of the Magi and the presence of God known in the blazing star; the baptism of Christ and the appearance of God in the form of a dove; and the miracle at Cana with God's presence coming to light by turning water into wine.

All three spoke to the physical presence of God in and through creation. All of these events are chapters in the story of how a helpless infant born in a Bethlehem stable brought salvation to the world. Epiphany is the extension of the Christmas story. The Holy Child in the manger was also the God who created the universe.

The Magi, representing the races of humanity, paid homage to the newborn Savior with gifts. Melchior brought gold, a royal gift celebrating Christ's role as Sovereign of the Jews and his dominion in this world. Casper brought frankincense, a fragrance that heralded the child's role as high priest. Balthasar brought myrrh, a symbol of the healing the Savior would bring to the world and the sorrows he would take on.

Who were the Magi in ancient times? The word itself is Indo-European in origin, meaning "great and illustrious." The Magi were a caste of priestly scholars who devoted themselves not only to the study of religion but to the natural sciences, medicine, astronomy, mathematics, and astrology. They devoted their lives to seeking wisdom. As in many cultures, both ancient and modern, the natural world was looked to as a way in which God's will was revealed. God spoke through the heavens and natural wonders.

The Old Testament is filled with other predictions and portents in which God's will is revealed to humankind through the heavens. In Genesis, we find Joseph dreaming about eleven stars bowing down to him. Numbers records that a star would rise from Jacob. A traditional prophecy used in interpreting the visit of the Magi is recorded in Isaiah: "Nations shall come to your light, and rulers to the brightness of your dawn" (Isa. 60:3). The prophet Joel tells the Israelites of a time when God would "show portents in the heavens and on the earth, blood and fire and columns of smoke" (Joel 2:30). This same prophecy was seen as being fulfilled on the day of Pentecost, as recorded in Acts.

These nights of bright lights are ritualized in Syria and in Lebanon. Epiphany Eve is observed as the Night of Destiny. Christians in these countries tell a legend that at midnight the trees miraculously bow down as a remembrance of the night when the trees bent down to show the Magi another way to go home, away from the terror and violence of Herod and toward the light and safety of the holy family. For Moslems in these countries, it is said that Al Loran came from heaven on this night, and all animals and trees bow down in honor of the revelation of the Word of God.

Magi, stars, and blessings: These are the images born in rituals that bear out the tradition of the Epiphany story. In medieval times, an Epiphany play called *The Feast of the Star* was performed outside churches. Three kings, crowned and clad in the finest fabrics, would ride on horseback followed by a large crowd. They would bring cups filled with myrrh, incense, and gold, offering the gifts before the Creator.

Children in England, Holland, France, Austria, Germany, and many Slavic countries continue to celebrate this procession in their neighborhoods. Epiphany songs are sung as young people go from house to house, carrying a pole with the star of Bethlehem attached. They share stories from their journey as Magi, and wish all a happy and holy Christmas.

The message of the Magi is further enacted with a house blessing, traditionally shared on January 6. Family members ask a minister to come to their home and bless it for the coming year. After a reading of the song of Mary, the rooms are sprinkled with water and incensed. Blessings of good health, chastity, humility, and goodness are pronounced. As the year and the initials of the three Magi are etched with chalk on the doorway, a blessing on all who enter is proclaimed: "All who enter these doorways may find your peace in the shelter of this home and seek your light as they journey forth."[1]

ENTERING THE STORY: IDEAS FOR FAMILY CELEBRATION

The extraordinary events of this season of celebrating God's coming into the world are drawing to a close. The stories of a star guiding the Magi, of angel choirs speaking to common laborers, of God entering the world as a helpless infant have now been told. We enter an ordinary time in the church year, a time where the story of God and God's creating Word need now become present in our day-to-day lives. But things never will be ordinary, because God has now entered the world. We are called to live in an ordinary world with this extraordinary news.

1. In the early morning light of this day, gather around the Christmas tree. Let the only light in the house be the light of the tree and a few candles. Rest in the silence of this time. Watch the candlelight dance or the ornaments reflect the lights on your tree.

   Breathe deeply. Let the events of the past twelve days flow through you. Breathe in the light of Christ, the refreshing breath of Jesus' presence in your life. Breathe out the shadows of moments or events in the past year where the light dimmed. Breathe in God's presence. Breathe out anything that separates you from that presence.

Read the scripture set aside for this day. As you read, pick out a word or phrase that speaks to you. If you are gathered as a group of friends or a family, share the words that spoke to you. If you are alone, write down the insights you were given in a journal or in a letter to a friend.

2. Go outside on a cloudless night. Find one bright star. Follow its movement through the evening and subsequent evenings as it travels across the sky.

3. Traditionally, this day is the day that Christmas decorations are removed. As a family unit, do this is such a way that it is not a mere housekeeping chore, but rather a celebratory way to close the season. Remember the story of how you got particular ornaments.

   Before the decorations are taken down, set aside a time after the meal or another intentional time to hear or read again the Epiphany text from Isaiah. Look around your home and decide what item should be left out for the season. The item may remind you of the light in the shadows, or the item may be a visual sign of the incarnation. Your family may choose any of the themes of the twelve days of Christmas to be upheld by the decoration left behind.

4. Celebrate this day as children of Europe do, with an Epiphany procession. Make a star from cardboard and leftover Christmas wrapping. Affix the star to the top of a broomstick. Gather family, friends, and other children, and follow the star through the neighborhood, stopping at neighbors' homes to sing the last Christmas carols of the season and wish them a good year.

5. Epiphany Eve is known as the Night of Destiny in Syria and Lebanon, when trees bow down in remembrance of the night they bent down to show the Magi the path away from the violence of Herod. We are living in a time of destiny, a time when humankind needs to make decisions that care for all of creation.

   Close your eyes and think about the shadows that cover the earth and the peoples of the earth. Imagine the places in your own life, your neighborhood, this country, and the world. Imagine the light of God's Word dawning on these areas. Form a prayer for those images and concerns. Devote one day a week to praying for the shadows that cover the earth. As an individual or family, find one environmental or social-justice activity or educational event in which you can participate to enlighten the world around you.

6. Go to the library and get a copy of the children's story about Le Befana. She was an elderly Italian woman who, legend says, was visited by the Magi on their way to find the Christchild. They asked her to go with them, but she decided to stay and finish her work. She later left and got lost. To this day, Le Befana's story is enacted in Italian communities as she leaves presents for children, in hopes of finding *Gesu Bambino*.

7. Celebrate Epiphany with three kings' cake. Before the cake is baked, place a coin in the batter. When the cake is served, the person who receives the piece of the cake that contains the coin is proclaimed one of the Magi. Let that person decide how he or she will lead the group toward the light throughout the rest of the season.

NOTES

---

1. Christmas Day

1. Fernard Cabrol, *The Year's Liturgy* (London: Burns, Oates & Wafbourne, 1938), 1:63.

2. The Feast of Stephen

1. The familiar carol "Good King Wenceslas" was written by John Mason Neale (1818–1866) using the tune PIAE CANTIONES (1582).

3. The Feast of Saint John

1. This story is based on "The Shoemaker's Tale," which was adapted by Leo Tolstoy, among other authors.

4. The Feast of the Holy Innocents

1. Philip H. Pfattiecher and Carlos R. Meserli, *The Manual on the Liturgy: Lutheran Book of Worship* (Minneapolis: Augsburg Fortress, 1979), 35.

6. The Women of Christmas

1. This story is based on a traditional Mexican Christmas tale, "The Legend of the Poinsettia," which speaks of the poinsettia as *flores de la Noche Buena* (flowers of the Good Night).

2. Mary Ann Simcoe, ed., *A Christmas Sourcebook* (Chicago: Liturgy Training Publications, 1984), 93.

11. And Heaven and Nature Sing

1. Our chapter title comes from the popular Christmas hymn "Joy to the World." It was written by Isaac Watts (1674–1748), with music by Lowell Mason (1792–1872). Watts based this hymn on Psalm 98, part of the morning scripture readings for Christmas Day.

2. Psalm 98 based on the New Revised Standard Version of the Bible, adapted in *The New Century Hymnal* (Cleveland, Ohio: The Pilgrim Press, 1995), 686.

12. The Blessing of the Waters

1. Thomas J. Talley, *The Origins of the Liturgical Year* (New York: Pueblo, 1986), 114.

2. Simcoe, *A Christmas Sourcebook,* 134.

3. Ibid., 136. This is an adaptation of the Great Blessing of Water in the Byzantine rite.

13. Epiphany

1. Gertrud Mueller Nelson, *To Dance with God: Family Ritual and Community Celebration* (Mahwah, N.J.: Paulist Press, 1986), 119.

SELECTED BIBLIOGRAPHY

Adam, Adolf. *The Liturgical Year: Its History and Its Meaning after the Reform of the Liturgy.* New York: Pueblo, 1981.

Cabrol, Fernard. *The Year's Liturgy. Vol. 1: Seasons.* London: Burns, Oates & Wafbourne, 1938.

Chambers, Robert, ed. *The Book of Days: A Miscellany of Popular Antiquities in Connection with the Calendar.* Philadelphia: J. B. Lippincott, 1891.

Gueranger, Abbot. *The Liturgical Year. Book II: Christmas.* Westminster, Md.: Newman Press, 1948.

Hall, Manly P. *The Story of Christmas.* Los Angeles: Philosophical Research Society, 1956.

Kneller, K. A. Heinrich. *Heortology: A History of the Christian Festivals from Their Origin to the Present Day.* London: Kegan Paul, Trench, Trubner, 1908.

McNeill, Leon A., and Angela A. Clendenin. *The Liturgical Year.* Wichita, Ks.: Catholic Action Committee, 1939.

Meeks, Blair Gilmer. *Liturgy: The Twelve Days* 12, no. 3 (winter 1995).

Metcalfe, Edna. *The Trees of Christmas.* Nashville, Tenn.: Abingdon Press, 1969.

Nelson, Gertrud Mueller. *To Dance with God: Family Ritual and Community Celebration.* Mahwah, N.J.: Paulist Press, 1986.

O'Carroll, Michael. *Theotokos: A Theological Encyclopedia of the Blessed Virgin Mary.* Wilmington, Del.: Michael Glazier, 1982.

O'Neal, Debbie Trafton. *Before and after Christmas: Activities and Ideas for Advent and Epiphany.* Illus. David LaRochelle. Minneapolis: Augsburg Fortress, 1991.

Pfattiecher, Philip H., and Carlos R. Meserli. *The Manual on the Liturgy: Lutheran Book of Worship.* Minneapolis: Augsburg Fortress, 1979.

Ramshaw, Gail. "Mary as the Symbol of Grace." In *Worship: Searching for Language.* Washington, D.C.: Pastoral Press, 1988.

Simcoe, Mary Ann, ed. *A Christmas Sourcebook.* Chicago: Liturgy Training Publications, 1984.

Spicer, Dorothy Gladys. *The Book of Festivals.* New York: Woman's Press, 1937.

Talley, Thomas J. *The Origins of the Liturgical Year.* New York: Pueblo, 1986.

Weiser, Francis X. *Handbook of Christian Feasts and Customs.* New York: Harcourt, Brace, 1958.

INDEX OF COUNTRIES OR CULTURAL ORIGINS

INDEX OF SCRIPTURES

The scriptures we use as a basis for our reflections on each day of the Christmas season are based on the readings from the *Revised Common Lectionary* for the appointed day, with two exceptions: from December 29–31, we follow the Christmas story to include the stories of Simeon and Anna; and on January 4, we substitute the use of Psalm 98, which is the psalm for Christmas Day and for morning prayer on December 31 and January 1. The translation we use is the New Revised Standard Version.